21 DAYS OF
PRAYER
and FASTING

ELMER TOWNS

DESTINY IMAGE® PUBLISHERS, INC.
P.O. Box 310, Shippensburg, PA 17257-0310
"Promoting Inspired Lives."

This book and all other Destiny Image and Destiny Image Fiction books are available at Christian bookstores and distributors worldwide.

For more information on foreign distributors, call 717-532-3040.

Reach us on the Internet: www.destinyimage.com.

ISBN 13 TP: 979-8-8815-0195-2

ISBN 13 eBook: 979-8-8815-0196-9

For Worldwide Distribution.

1 2 3 4 5 6 7 8 / 29 28 27 26 25 24

TABLE OF CONTENTS

PART FIVE

PART ONE

HOW TO FAST

INTRODUCTION

I believe in fasting because of what I have seen it do in my personal life. I learned to fast from my pastor, Jerry Falwell. In the spring of 1972, he led us to fast for great numerical growth at Thomas Road Baptist Church, and we saw the altars filled with lost people coming to Christ. But they were not just numbers added to the church roll. I saw alcoholics transformed; not only did they quit drinking, but they become passionate witnesses in their homes and communities.

During that same fast, we asked God for one million dollars. The church reached that goal. In 1978, we fasted and prayed for five million dollars to build seven dorms on Liberty University's property. The money came in weekly, and we occupied the dorms in September of that year.

In 1994, I saw Jerry Falwell fast for 52 million dollars to pay off tremendous university debts and keep the university out of bankruptcy. He fasted 40 days drinking only water and Diet Pepsi (he said there was no protein in colored water). During those 40 days, God kept telling him, "Find My heart, not My pocketbook." When the money did not come in, Falwell ate normally for the next 25 days. During those 25 days, he did what he humanly could to solve our problem. Then God told him to fast again, so he began fasting for another 40 days. Five days after he finished the second 40-day fast, Falwell phoned me to come to his office to meet a courier who brought 25 million dollars in a check and 27 million in collateral to cover all our indebtedness. The greatest answer to prayer I had ever seen!

Fasting is not just a spiritual exercise when you are in trouble or face a crisis, and fasting is not just getting things from God. Fasting is a relationship with God when you sacrificially put aside food to spend quality time with your Savior. You fast because He is the most important Person in your life. He is more important than the food you enjoy or any other thing that gets in the way of prayer.

Fasting is your life-statement of praise to God. You magnify Him by making a statement that God is more important than eating.

Fasting is your love-relationship to God. You are telling God—the One you should love the most—that He is more important than food. You come off food for a determined length of time so you can spend time with Him.

Fasting is your worship—commitment to your Lord and Savior. Doesn't the word *worship* come from the old Scottish word "worthship"? Therefore, when you fast you are demonstrating to God that He is "worth" everything to you. He is preeminent... the holy One...the only One in your life who owns you and directs you. God is "worth" giving up food, entertainment, or anything else. Paul said, "That I may know [Christ] and the power of His resurrection" (Phil. 3:10, NKJV).

Fasting is a faith-expression to God that you believe He exists and that He will do for you what He promises. When you fast, you make Him number one in your life (Heb. 11:6).

Chapter one is designed to introduce beginners to fasting and get them started.

Chapter two explains the six types of fasting and suggest when to use each fast. Second, it also explains the various purposes of fasting.

Chapter three helps you learn how to fast to know God and worship Him. In one sense, you should praise God and worship Him every time you fast and pray. But for certain fasts you will want to focus primarily on praise and worship. Essentially, God should be your focus every time you pray. But there will be seasons when you dedicated your entire schedule to praise and worship. It's hard to explain, but once you have experienced worship, you experience His presence.

The third section features 21 days of daily devotions. As you read, let God talk with you, and then you talk to God about the issues for that day/week. What you read about fasting in the chapters of this book, talk with God about those same issues.

Finally, there's an appendix that answers some of the questions you may have about fasting. Some readers go to this section first to answer any issues they may have with fasting.

As I have challenged in many other places, reach out and touch God as you read and examine the events and deceptions of this book. But more importantly, may God reach out to touch you.

Writing from my home on top of Liberty Mountain,

Elmer Towns

Chapter 1

WHAT FASTING IS AND HOW TO GET STARTED

MY wife Ruth and I were struggling to make two house payments: one in Lynchburg, Virginia, where we had moved to found Liberty University, and one in Chicago, our previous home that had not yet sold. I told my wife, "Let's fast for the house to sell." We had never fasted before. The house payment in Chicago was due the fifteenth of the month, so we fasted on that date (a Yom Kippur one-day fast, we did not eat but prayed during the evening meal, breakfast and lunch). Nothing happened. A month later, we did the same thing, and again nothing happened. The process went on for six months, and then we finally received an offer to purchase.

I went to Chicago for the closing, and the buyer told me he had begun looking at my house on his wife's birthday. I did not think anything of it until he told me his wife's birthday was six months ago on the sixteenth—the day after our first fast. The hair on the back of my neck stood up, and I froze in fear. What if we had not fasted? Then he told me he had come back around the fifteenth of each month to look at the house, trying to make a decision. I asked myself, "What if we had not continued to fast on the fifteenth of every month while he was looking?"

That first fast taught me three important lessons. First, fasting takes your prayers to a higher level to get answers. Second, when you fast with someone else, you are agreeing together (see Matt. 18:19). Third, once you start fasting, do not quit. God may have begun to answer your prayers. If you quit fasting it is possible God will quit the process of answering your prayers.

Since that time, I have made fasting a part of my Christian lifestyle. I fast for big requests as well as for small ongoing needs.

Your body is a finely tuned physical engine that needs fuel to use its enormous power. That fuel is called *food*. To make sure your body gets the fuel it needs, God created an appetite within you to eat. Your appetite to eat is satisfied by food. God built within you an eating cycle to give you energy and keep you living.

So why would you choose to deliberately break this cycle?

Starvation is a worldwide challenge. We have all seen pictures of little children with swollen bellies and hungry children begging for something to eat with empty cups. Starving people stampede when a food truck arrives in refugee villages. People trample on one another just to get a slice of bread. While so many in the world are clamoring for food, why would you voluntarily give up eating?

Around the world, many people are glad to get one meal a day. But Americans are culturally programmed to eat three daily "square" meals. Haven't you heard, "Breakfast is the most important meal of the day"? Did your mother ever tell you, "Eat so you'll grow up strong"? She also said to get some exercise to stay fit and to bundle up on cold days to stay healthy. Great advice! But that brings us to another question.

Will you be healthy if you do not eat?

Our television screens are filled with commercials for diet pills, diet programs and exercise equipment, all promising to help you develop a strong, healthy body and lose some weight. As the world glorifies and idolizes a healthy body, why would we sacrifice basic food?

Some people cut back on food to lose weight for health reasons or for the vanity of having a trim body. Is it really that outrageous to consider fasting for a spiritual purpose? Consider people with high blood pressure who stop eating fried foods and fatty desserts to save themselves from a stroke. What is wrong with a person who fasts to save herself spiritually? Just as a diabetic avoids sweets to prevent a negative insulin reaction, you may enter a partial fast to keep your walk with God your first priority.

There are many ways to sacrifice your strength. If you sacrifice your strength by working for God all day at a church outreach event, is that any different than sacrificing your strength in fasting? Not really. In both instances, God sees our sacrifice and rewards according to the faith of our hearts.

Most Christians in America do not fast. It's not part of the liturgy of high churches, and many congregational churches do not practice it. Yet Jesus assumed it as part of a healthy prayer life: *"When* you fast . . ."* (Matt. 6:16, emphasis added). Why? Perhaps Jesus knew that we would not get an answer to our prayers until we demonstrate our humility and sincerity by fasting. When we give up that which is enjoyable—food—we are telling God that we sincerely trust Him to answer our prayer. You demonstrate your sincerity when you give up food, which is necessary for strength and vitality. When you are willing to sacrifice by fasting, God sees your faith and answers your prayer.

There are many godly people who have never fasted and yet receive frequent answers to prayer. For example, every church has a godly grandmother who is an extremely effective intercessor. Many of those godly grandmas have never fasted. Why are they so effective in prayer? Effective intercessors live continuously close to God. While the average Christian needs the discipline of fasting in order to pray effectively, the grandmother stays in God's presence and doesn't need discipline for effective intercession.

By way of illustration, imagine two men who want to keep in shape physically. One man goes to the gym every day and works out on all the equipment. His discipline has made him a perfect specimen of health and strength. The second man has never been to the gym and would not know the first thing about using free weights or a rowing machine. But he works in construction. Every day, he slings a hammer, lifts heavy materials and climbs around on scaffolding. His occupation has made him a perfect specimen of health and strength.

Great intercessors are like that. They are occupied by prayer in God's presence on a daily basis, strong and healthy in heart and soul. But most of us are like the first man. We need the discipline of fasting to keep us spiritually fit and strong.

THE YOM KIPPUR FAST

When should a fast begin? When should it end? In the Old Testament, we find instructions for every Jew to fast on Yom Kippur, the Day of Atonement. "On the tenth day of the seventh month of each year, you must go without eating" (Lev. 16:29, CEV). Those who fast for Yom Kippur refrain from eating the evening meal, breakfast and lunch.

Why does the fast begin in the evening rather than in the morning? God measures a day differently than we do. "The evening and the morning were the first day" (Gen. 1:5, NKJV). While we think of day as daylight, God thinks of a day as a 24-hour period that begins at the end of daylight, or the beginning of the night. The Yom Kippur fast begins at sundown, continues for 24 hours and is broken at sundown the following day at the evening meal.

A Jewish guide in Israel was asked if he kept the Yom Kippur fast. He replied, almost belligerently, "Certainly, I am a good Jew. I do not eat the evening meal, breakfast or lunch."

Then he was asked at what time he breaks his fast to eat the evening meal.

He threw his head back and laughed, whiskers bouncing on his face. "The rabbi tells us not to break our fast until we can see two stars in the sky." Then he said with a sly wink, "A hungry Jewish man may see one star that's not really there, so he must wait until he sees two." He looked to the sky and bellowed, "And I pray that Yom Kippur does not have a cloudy night!"

You may decide to wait until two stars appear in the evening sky or to eat the evening meal at whatever time it is normally served. The important point is to give your fasting day or days a full 24 hours, beginning and ending at the evening meal.

FASTING BASICS

If you have never fasted, it may be scary to think about not eating—and even scarier after you start fasting. A few hours after you have skipped your first meal you feel hunger pains, and nothing inspires doubt like hunger! Maybe this was not such a good idea after all. You can turn these moments of anxiety to work in your favor. When hunger pains hit, that is a perfect reminder to pray for the request that brought you to fasting in the first place.

Some people do not attempt to fast because they believe they lack the willpower to withhold food. But the ability to stay on a fast has nothing to do with successfully avoiding food. The power to fast comes from a thirst to be in God's presence and a hunger for answered prayer. So, do not try "tricks" to keep you on the fast. Some people walk around with a bottle of water to sip or a stick of gum to chew every time they think of food. If you use tricks like these, you are paying attention to the least important aspect of fasting. Focus your attention on the Lord Jesus Christ, not on the fact that you are not eating. Claim the promise, "I can do everything through Christ, who gives me strength" (Phil. 4:13, NLT).

Others worry that fasting could cause health problems. Many of us think of our bodies like cars: If we do not put oil in the engine, it'll burn up. A one-day fast from solid food is like driving a car with the oil warning light on. A 21-day Daniel fast (vegetables only) is like going on a cross-country road trip without enough water, oil or gas. But most people find that, rather than causing harm, fasts have a positive effect on their health. When you fast, you eliminate poisons and toxins from your body; the longer your fast, the more toxins and potential diseases are eliminated. Many who fast find their blood pressure has gone down, along with their cholesterol. (If you have a health condition that might be affected by withholding food or changing your diet, see your doctor before you begin. He or she will advise you how to avoid harming your health during your fast.)

Some people ask, "What will my friends think if I don't eat with them?" The answer is simple: You don't fast to impress your friends. Have you ever gone to a restaurant with an upset stomach and ordered just a ginger ale? Other times you ordered only coffee. You didn't care what your friends thought then. When you fast, just order a beverage and don't worry what your friends think. On most occasions, you don't even need to let your friends know you are fasting.

Jesus commanded His followers, "When you fast, don't make it obvious, as the hypocrites do, for they try to look pale and disheveled so people will admire them for their fasting. But when you fast, comb your hair and wash your face. Then no one will notice that you are fasting, except your Father, who knows what you do in private. And your Father, who sees everything, will reward you" (Matt. 6:16-18, NLT). What do these verses mean for us? God does not look at the outward activity of fasting; God looks at our heart. The outward act of fasting does not make us extra spiritual or special "people of God." More significant to God is the inward attitude that motivates our fast.

Sometimes you fast privately, not telling anyone—including your spouse. At other times, you share your fast with others and you agree together to seek a request of God. "If two of you agree here on earth concerning anything you ask, my Father in heaven will do it for you" (Matt. 18:19, NLT). We read in Scripture of many times when people agreed to fast together. Ezra fasted with 4,000 people when they faced a dangerous trip from Babylon back to Jerusalem (Ezra 8:21-23). Esther asked all the Jews in Persia to fast with her for divine intervention before she went to see the king (Esth. 4:16). Shirley Dobson and Vonette Bright appeared before a House Committee in Washington, D.C., to testify for the passage of a National Day of Prayer and fasting. On the first Thursday of each May, tens of thousands of people agree in prayer to ask God's mercy and blessing on the United States, its leaders and its people.

When you fast, expect resistance. A friend may call you goofy, while others keep their negative thoughts to themselves. You may even find some "good ol' soul" who tries to talk you out of fasting. But your fast is not about them; it is between you and God. Don't break your vow, even under pressure. Satan will oppose you. He doesn't want you in the presence of God interceding for spiritual victory! He wants to destroy you and will not easily give up territory he has conquered. "Stay alert! Watch out for your great enemy, the devil. He prowls around like a roaring lion, looking for someone to devour" (1 Pet. 5:8, NLT).

KEEP CLIMBING!

Fasting is not easy. It is both a physical and spiritual challenge. It can be difficult, draining and dangerous. But it is worth the trouble! It's like climbing a mountain. Make a vow and begin climbing to your destination. Your body may say, "You can't climb any higher, you need rest." It's okay to rest, but don't break your fast in the midst of your climb. If you quit halfway through, you won't win the victory God wants to give you. If you sit down and relax for a while, that's alright. But don't start eating. Rest awhile and then start climbing again, all the way to the top.

Begin your fast with full knowledge that the path ahead may be tough. Acknowledge that you may be tempted to quit. But keep your goal in mind: the top of the mountain. When you get there, you'll see something very few people have seen.

There's a story that all the young boys of a certain Native American tribe had to climb to the top of the mountain in order to become warriors, worthy to fight alongside the other men. Some of the young boys quit halfway up, and they never attained full manhood. Other boys came back claiming they had been to the top. The chief asked each one, "What did you see?" Their answers revealed who was a worthy warrior and who was not. The chief knew the young men had been to the top when they answered, "I saw something I had never seen before; I saw the sea."

Keep climbing. You do not climb alone—God's presence is with you every step of the way. And answers you have never seen or even imagined await you at the summit. When you honestly fast, you will meet God and He will meet you.

HOW TO BEGIN FASTING

The decision to fast is like leaves on a head of lettuce. Just as there are many layers of lettuce leaves, so there are many layers to the decision process. The first and outer leaf is a wish. Fasting is something you've thought about doing, but not very seriously. Then you hear a challenge from the pulpit or a friend or a book and think, "That would be nice or perhaps I need to fast to get a specific prayer answered." You begin to wish you could touch God through prayer and fasting. That's good. For when you do it properly, God will touch you.

The second leaf is desire. You go beyond a casual wish to a deep longing. You think about fasting two or three times a day, driving to work or during other quiet moments. When you think about spending intense, deliberate time with God, your heart hungers to begin. The more you think about fasting, the more you become convinced you could do it. You say to yourself: I want to touch God through fasting, and I won't be satisfied until I do it.

The third leaf is determination. You begin to tell yourself: I know I can last through a one-day fast. You think back to times when you skipped a meal, or even two meals in a day. The idea of fasting is no longer strange or overly intimidating—in fact, fasting has begun to sound like a very good idea indeed. The more you think about it, the more you are determined to go a whole day without eating.

The fourth leaf is planning. You might begin to write your prayer list or to focus on your church's prayer project. You might plan to read one or two (or three) Christian books you have wanted to read for years but have never had the opportunity. You plan the place where you will pray and begin thinking through how you will manage your schedule.

The fifth leaf is something psychologists call imprinting. When you imprint, the decision becomes a part of you, and you become a part of the decision. You have decided, "Yes, I can and will do it." You know you can pray and get the answers you seek. You know you can touch God, and you are ready to start.

The sixth leaf is launching. This is when you actually begin your first fast. When you launch, your focus is not on missing a meal; you are looking forward to meeting with God. You retreat to your private place and begin praying. Your prayer list is there, your devotional book is ready, and your heart anticipates the experience. You've prepared and are ready to meet God.

The final and inner leaf is the presence of God. When you begin fasting with the Lord's Prayer, your first petition is "Hallowed be Thy name." When you pray for God's name to be hallowed, you are crying out, "Holy! Holy! Holy!" Your prayer is an act of worship. And when you worship, God comes to receive it. Jesus said the Father is seeking worshipers who will worship in the Spirit and in truth (see John 4:23). When you fast and pray in faith, you are the kind of worshiper the Father seeks—and His presence will find you in your place of prayer and worship.

You will find there's power in the presence of God. Imagine dozens of freight cars pulled by one engine. Car after car, one after another, takes its journey toward its destination—all because of the relentless, perpetual power of the engine. Like those freight cars, you will find it easy to miss meal after meal because of the power of God's presence. You will find prayer time following prayer time because of the power of God's presence. And you will find answered prayer upon answered prayer because of the power of God's presence.

Deepen your wish into a desire to fast. Determine and plan to fast. Become imprinted with your decision and then launch your fast. The presence of God awaits you.

LYNN'S STORY

A junior high-age girl at Thomas Road Baptist Church in Lynchburg, Virginia, heard her pastor and church leaders talk about fasting. The church adults, as well as the students at Liberty University, had been called to fast, but children had not been included.

Lynn worked on the puppet team in the Sunday night youth group. The group was planning a gospel presentation at a local juvenile detention center, and their leaders challenged them to pray that God would use them to turn young peoples' heart to Him. The ministry team of 13, counting all the puppeteers, singers and speakers, agreed together to pray. Lynn also decided to fast.

She decided on a Yom Kippur fast (24 hours from sundown to sundown). On the afternoon she began her fast, she went straight to the kitchen for a snack when she got home from school, reminding her mother of her plan to fast beginning at sundown. She didn't eat the evening meal. Instead, she went to her room and read some passages of Scripture and a chapter in a Christian book, and then went through her puppet presentation. (Her puppet had only a minor speaking part, but she considered herself vital to the total presentation.)

The next morning, Lynn didn't eat breakfast or lunch. She had a big glass of orange juice for breakfast and then went to school. Her mother had written permission for her teacher to allow Lynn to remain at her desk during lunch period.

"It was hard," Lynn confessed. "All I could think about all day was the fact I was not eating." In her 12-year old innocence, she confessed, "I could hardly wait until the sun went down so I could go to the kitchen and get a glass of milk and a half of a sandwich before dinner!" Then she smiled and continued, "I didn't cheat, I kept my fast the whole time."

For a 12-year old girl to go without eating for a whole day may seem like a simple thing, but after the puppet show at the juvenile home, several boys prayed to receive Christ. Many of the students on the ministry team rejoiced that God had used them, but without telling anyone or taking credit, Lynn knew God answered their prayers because she had fasted.

SIMPLE PREPARATIONS

If you are a newcomer to fasting, a one-day fast is the best place to start, just as it was for Lynn. You may have a pressing need or a deep thirst for God— or both—that tempt you to jump into the deep end and fast for a week or longer. But fasting is a lot like long-distance running. To run a marathon, you first must be able to run one mile. And if you haven't run one mile in a very long time (or ever!), it will take time for your body to become conditioned to the new rigors you are asking of it. And consider the likely consequences: If you start with a long fast and don't make it to the end, you may never fast again. But a successful one-day fast leads naturally to a successful three-day fast.

God is more concerned about your faith than He is about the length of your fast, or what food you give up, or other mechanical details. Giving up food is an indication of the attitude of your heart, and that is what God sees and measures.

Remember when Jesus observed people standing on the street corner making a great show of their prayers? He saw through them to the hypocrisy of their hearts. To His followers, He said, "When you pray, you shall not be like the hypocrites, for they love to pray standing in the synagogue and on the corners of the streets, that they may be seen by men... When you pray, do not use vain repetitions as the heathen do, for they think that they will be heard for their many words" (Matt. 6:5,7, NKJV). God hears and answers your prayers not because of how long you pray, or how loud you pray, or any other physical demonstration of sincerity. It's not the outward show, but the faith of the heart that counts.

When a man proposes to a woman, it's not the length of the proposal that is important, nor is it the eloquence of his words. In our modern day, young men propose in sensational ways such as climbing to the top of a mountain or skyscraper or proposing in front of an entire football stadium. These outward extravagances create memories, but what really counts is her "Yes!"

When you begin fasting, don't measure your success by the sensational things you do but by the sincerity of your heart. Your success in fasting is not measured by what you accomplish (God is the one who will accomplish your answered prayers), but by the faith that leads you to fast. Trust that God sees your full measure of faith and start at the beginning.

Keep it simple. When the sun goes down, or perhaps a little before the sun sets, begin to withhold food and to pray. Fasting is not just going without food. It is a deliberate, focused way of praying. Jesus told His followers that some prayers could only be answered when accompanied by fasting (see Matt. 17:2). His assumption is that we will pray when we fast, not just skip a few meals. So, pray!

At mealtime, go to your quiet place (your study, bedroom or other private location) and pray for the project for which you are fasting. A meal usually lasts anywhere from 30 to 60 minutes, but many people can't pray that long when they are just beginning to fast. Pray for a while, then read your Bible or a chapter in a devotional book that encourages you to more faith. Spend some time in worshipful meditation. Turn your thoughts to God by listening to and singing Christian music.

Follow the same sequence when you skip breakfast the following morning. Find a quiet place and spend approximately 30 minutes praying, studying the Bible and reading Christian literature. Follow the same pattern for lunchtime. If you have an office, close the door and spend that time with God. If you work outside, pray in your car or pickup truck, under a shady tree or on a walk, or in some other private place. Follow the same sequence of prayer, Bible study and Christian literature, accompanied by Christian music.

When Jerry Falwell called his church and the students at Liberty University to fast, he would announce, "Eat a small snack before you come to church on Sunday evening. We will begin fasting together during the Sunday evening service, and you'll not eat until the sun goes down on Monday. If you go out to fellowship with others after church, don't eat any solid food, just have something to drink." It was important to him that we not break our fast until the sun went down on Monday evening.

Falwell always thought Sunday night was the best time to start a fast. After all, he said, we had been in the house of God all day Sunday, nourished by His Word. I usually begin my private fasts on Monday. There is no "right" day to start. Choose a day that will work with your work, family and church schedules.

Why did Falwell tell his congregation to eat a snack on Sunday afternoon? Because there are instances in the Old Testament when God told His people to prepare for a fast by eating. For example, God called Elijah to a 40-day fast and told him, "Arise and eat, because the journey is too great for you" (1 Kings 19:7, NKJV). And what happened? "So, he (Elijah) arose, and ate and drank; and he went in the strength of that food forty days and forty nights as far as Horeb, the mountain of God" (1 Kings 19:8, NKJV).

Like Elijah and young Lynn from the puppet ministry, you may find that a simple afternoon snack before sundown helps you fulfill God's call to fast.

FAST WITH A PURPOSE

Before you fast, search your heart to determine the reason you are fasting. The best way to search your heart is to write down the purpose of your fast. There's an old adage that goes, "Thoughts disentangle themselves over lips and fingertips." Sometimes our written purpose perfectly reflects our heart. But other times, our thinking is not very clear. By changing the words or rewriting the sentence, you can sharpen and bring focus to your purpose. You may have three or four reasons why you are fasting. Write down each and determine which is the most important, putting them in order of priority. If you don't write them down, your objectives may remain blurred or vague. But when you put your purpose in writing, you know exactly what's at stake.

A fast is not easy. It's spiritual warfare. When you fast and pray, you take on the forces of hell. Even Satan's demons will try to stop you. Assume the attitude that you're going to war and have a clear objective for your battle.

When young David went to fight Goliath, he knew why he was fighting: "Is there not a cause?" (1 Sam. 17:29, NKJV). The other soldiers tried to stop David from fighting Goliath. Not only would they not fight the giant, they gave David all kinds of reasons why he should not fight the huge Philistine. Like those Israelite soldiers, friends may try to talk you out of your fast. But if you know why you are fasting, you can say with David, "Is there not a cause?"

What you're about to do is more than giving up food. It's more than spending time on your knees. God has called you to a higher purpose. You're fasting for a cause. When the battle becomes intense, knowing your cause will help you stay the course with purpose and sincerity.

On page 18 is a fasting checklist. Just as a pilot goes through a flight checklist before takeoff to ensure her plane arrives safely at its destination, so your checklist will help you complete your fast successfully. The pilot already knows to do the tasks on the list but checking off the items one by one gives her confidence to fly. Wouldn't you like to pray with confidence?

PLAN YOUR FAST

Do not enter into your fast casually. When you go on a driving vacation, you plan a route, where you will lodge and perhaps even where you will stop for meals. You might even make a budget. Take the same approach with fasting. Write out your plans, including your destination, how you will get there, where you will pray and what you will do during mealtimes.

A FAST IS A VOW

On your checklist, there is a vow for you to sign. This is not a legalistic document; it is covenant between you and God. You are making a commitment to seek the Lord and entreat His blessing on your life.

"I hope I can make it through" is not a vow. Neither is "I think I can make this work." No, a vow is a commitment in heart, mind and soul to the completion of the project. You are asking for God's presence, and you are entering into partnership with God to meet your need. According to Paul, "We are labourers together with God" (1 Cor. 3:9, KJV). Isn't it wonderful to be a co-laborer with God?

Your vow is not a bargain with God. There are some people who wrongly think they can "make a deal." It goes something like this: "God, if I don't eat for three days, will you heal my friend's cancer?" Fasting is nothing like a deal. It's not a transaction. That's legalism!

You are fasting based on the grace of God. In His grace, God forgives our sins because we cry out to Him in the name of Jesus Christ, not because we do good works to earn salvation. In the same way, we cry out in prayer and fasting for God's grace to answer our prayers. A vow to fast is a promise to trust God's grace to sustain your physical needs through your fast and to answer your prayer. When you sign a vow, you are saying that God is going to do it all and that you will accept whatever answer He sends. You are promising to trust that God, in His grace, will give you what is best.

If you have made a plan and filled out your checklist, you're almost ready to begin.

FASTING CHECKLIST

Purpose:

____

Fast: What you will withhold

____

Begin: Date _________________________ Time _________________________

End: Date _________________________ Time _________________________

Vow: I believe God is the only answer to my request and that prayer without fasting is not enough to get an answer to my need. Therefore, by faith I am fasting because I need God to work in this matter.

Bible Basis: My Bible promise

____

____

Resources: What I need during this fast

____

____

With God being my strength and grace being my basis, I commit myself to the above fast.

____
Signed   Date

Chapter 2

HOW TO GO ABOUT FASTING

TYPES, PURPOSES, AND DESCRIPTIONS

Fasting begins in the heart with a passion to know God. And because hunger for God is its wellspring, fasting is rarely a one-time event. Rather, for many believers, it becomes a regular habit in their vibrant pursuit of God. But not everybody fasts in the same way; in fact, many believers fast in different ways at different times. The reason is simple.

The Bible doesn't lay out rules on how to fast. It offers no formulas for fasting. Instead, Scripture describes what various believers do when they have a passion to know God. As a result, we see people fasting in many different ways, doing many different things—and the things they do are not always consistent. If we take the full testimony of Scripture, we must conclude there is no single correct way to fast. We find instead that God is not as concerned with the way we fast as He is with our attitude when we fast.

Whichever method you choose, approach your fast in humble trust that God will meet your needs.

SIX WAYS TO FAST

1. The "Normal" or Juice Fast

In the "normal" fast, individuals stop eating solid food. A biblical example of the normal fast is Yom Kippur: "On the tenth day of the seventh month of each year, you must go without eating to show sorrow for your sins" (Lev. 16:29, CEV). The Bible indicates that some people drank liquids during the fast, but it doesn't tell us what they drank. It may have been water, milk, the juice of various fruits or a liquid form of desert cacti.

Hence, people who undertake a normal fast today have freedom to decide what liquids they will drink while they fast from solid food.

The normal fast usually lasts for one day, three days or a week. Longer fasts are possible but should be undertaken only after plenty of practice with shorter fasts. Remember, you must train to run a marathon! After many years of shorter fasts, I once fasted for 40 days by drinking a glass of orange juice in the morning and a glass of V8 juice in the evening. During the day, I drank water and coffee.

I have been criticized for drinking coffee during a fast because it is a stimulant. To me, coffee is just the liquid I drink in the morning! When I fast, I drink a hot cup around six A.M., then I keep coffee on my desk to sip throughout the morning hours. About once an hour, I take a sip of coffee—even after it's cold. At that point, I'm not drinking coffee because I like it or because it is a stimulant. I'm drinking it to keep my mouth and throat moist! To those who criticize drinking coffee during a fast, I offer the following reminder: God is more concerned about the prayers that come out of our hearts than He is about the liquid that goes into our bodies.

Whether you choose fruit and vegetable juices, milk, coffee or tea, or water only, decide in advance what liquids you will allow during your fast. Use your fasting checklist to ensure you have supplied yourself with the resources you will need to stay both hydrated and committed.

2. The Absolute Fast

When they undertake an absolute fast, people do not eat solid food or drink liquids of any kind. No one should ever follow an absolute fast for more than two or three days. Medical authorities say that after six or seven days with no liquid, your physical organs shut down. That is, you die. But long before that seven days are up; you'll do permanent damage to your brain. Water is essential to life and you cannot survive without it.

Three days is the limit for an absolute fast. If you decide to undertake this kind of fast, drink plenty of water in the days leading up to your launch. This will help to ensure you stay hydrated and healthy for the one, two or three days you are fasting. You should also be sensible about your activities during your fast. Don't work out or play sports or do any other activity that causes you to sweat heavily or get overheated. When your body sweats, it loses water that must be replenished—something you have vowed not to do! Fasting is demanding enough for your body. Don't overtax it with activities that can wait until your fast is complete.

3. The Daniel Fast

The Daniel fast is sometimes called a partial fast. In this fast, certain foods are omitted or certain foods are eaten on a modified schedule. Those who fast in this way may also abstain from certain activities.

As a young Hebrew man, Daniel was taken as an exile from conquered Judah to Babylon, where he was "retrained" to serve in the court of Nebuchadnezzar. Part of his retraining was a special diet designed to acculturate Jewish young men into the Babylonian culture. The goal was for the Jewish exiles to live by Babylonian laws, values and customs, and to eat Babylonian food. "The king assigned them a daily ration of food and wine from his own kitchens. They were to be trained for three years, and then they would enter the royal service" (Dan. 1:5, NLT).

Daniel and his friends asked to be excused from eating the meat and drinking the wine (see Dan. 1:11-14). The Bible says, "Daniel purposed in his heart that he would not defile himself with the portion of the king's delicacies, nor with the wine" (Dan. 1:8, NKJV). The secret to Daniel's successful fast was his vow not to eat what the king provided.

Why did Daniel ask to be excused? Scripture does not say. Perhaps the food had been offered to idols and eating it would legitimize the Babylonian gods. Perhaps the wine was highly intoxicating and drinking it would lead to drunkenness. Perhaps the food included non-kosher meats which violated Jewish dietary laws. Perhaps he merely had a desire for good health, but it seems more likely that he wanted to keep his body separate to God. (Isn't that one of the reasons you fast?) Whatever the case, Daniel knew that Babylonian food and drink was off-limits. He did not want to compromise his way of life, which was dedicated to honoring Yahweh, for a new culture.

So, what did Daniel do? The young man said to his trainers, "Prove thy servants, I beseech thee, ten days; and let them give us pulse to eat, and water to drink" (Dan. 1:12, KJV). Most of the newer translations use the word *vegetables* instead of *pulse*. The original Hebrew word probably refers to leafy vegetables such as lettuce, turnip greens, cabbage, spinach and so on. Daniel went on a salad diet! And what happened? "At the end of ten days their features appeared better and fatter in flesh than all the young men who ate the portion of the king's delicacies" (Dan. 1:15, NKJV).

While Daniel's first fast in Babylon was for 10 days, he later fasted for 21 days (see Dan. 10). Because of the prophet's example, what we call the Daniel fast is a time fast for a specific purpose. (The purpose of Daniel's 10-day fast was to prove God's sufficiency to his trainers; his second was to receive a vision from God; see Dan. 10:1-3.)

The Daniel Fast is a *time vow*, so you need to decide ahead of time how long you will fast and then be firm to that commitment to the end. Because I've written several books on fasting, I receive letters from people who tell me about their experiences with fasting. On occasion, some individuals will tell me that they are on the 42nd day of a 40-day fast and are enjoying the experience so much that they don't want to stop. They ask, "What should I do?" I write back and tell them to stop immediately. Their fast was a *time vow*. They should begin on time, keep the promise to fast the entire time, and end on time.

The Daniel Fast is also a *discipline vow*. You strengthen your character in every area of your life when you fulfill your Daniel Fast. When you take control of your body—your outer self—you begin to take control of your inner character. You discipline your body to glorify the Lord.

The Daniel Fast is a *spiritual commitment*. You pray while fasting for a *spiritual goal*. Remember, fasting will not accomplish much without serious, sacrificial prayer. As you discipline your body, you are disciplining your prayer life.

The Daniel Fast is a *faith vow*. In Mark 11:22 (NKJV), Jesus exhorted His disciples, "Have faith in God." To explain how they could express their faith, He directed them, "Whoever says to this mountain [problem or goal], 'Be removed and be cast into the sea,' and does not doubt in his heart, but believes that those things he says will be done, he will have whatever he says" (v. 23). When Daniel began his fast, he made a statement of faith to eat only vegetables and drink water. Likewise, your fast is a verbal statement of what you want God to do.

The Daniel Fast is a *partial vow*. You don't give up all food (an absolute fast), nor do you go on just a juice fast (a normal fast). Instead, you omit certain foods that you would typically eat or eliminate certain meals for a specified period of time. This may include omitting one or two meals a day for a certain length of time, or it may involve omitting other practices.

The Daniel Fast is a *healthy vow*. You abstain from "party" food, or junk food. Usually, you don't eat between meals, and you only eat healthy foods.

Finally, the Daniel Fast is a *lifestyle vow*. When Daniel asked permission to avoid the king's delicacies for 10 days, he put his whole life into his chosen diet. Then, if he continued to look "healthy," he could continue following his own diet.

Some who take a vow against alcoholic beverages take a lifelong vow—they commit to never taste alcoholic drinks again. They may make this vow for health reasons, because alcohol consumption can lead to cirrhosis of the liver and premature death. Some make the vow because of addiction to alcohol—they have been a slave to it. Still others vow not to taste alcohol for spiritual reasons, because they believe drinking alcohol is wrong. (My father died an alcoholic, and my family suffered poverty and other problems because of his addiction. I have read the Scriptures closely and personally I conclude that drinking in any form is wrong.) In the Bible, John the Baptist, the prophet Samuel, and Samson made lifelong vows to avoid alcohol. If we want to honor the Lord as they did, we should follow their example in their Nazirite vow (see Num. 6:1-8).

In the record of Daniel's 21-day fast, he said, "I ate no pleasant food, no meat or wine came into my mouth" (Dan. 10:3, NKJV). The word translated "pleasant food" in this verse probably means things we consider enjoyable, such as steak broiled over an open fire, escargot, veal cutlets with provolone, or a baked Alaska. The NIV translates these words as "choicest food"; the CEV calls it "fancy food"; the CSV and the TLB use "rich food." The Daniel fast is giving up things you enjoy while you eat or doing only what is necessary. Here are some different ways the Daniel fast is celebrated:

- Eat one meal a day and spend the other mealtimes in prayer. Perhaps they are thinking of Jesus' exhortation, "Could you not watch with Me one hour?" (Matt. 26:40, NKJV). It takes about one hour to eat a meal served in a restaurant or eaten at home, so one hour of prayer and meditation is recommended for each skipped meal.
- Eat only vegetables. Daniel gave up all other food groups except vegetables. While this is a good fast, it doesn't set aside time to pray. It assumes that you will eat vegetables at mealtime and pray at other times during the day.
- Give up television for a limited time. Unsaved people may hear you have given up television and laugh at you. But this is a commitment of time: You're going to take back the hours you spend in front of the TV and instead spend time with God. It's also a spiritual fast, practicing putting Christ first. "Seek first the kingdom of God and His righteousness, and all these things shall be added to you" (Matt. 6:33, NKJV).
- Give up sports for a limited time. Participation in sports is good for us, not only because it helps keep us fit but also because it can help us grow in character when we practice teamwork and good sportsmanship. However, giving up participation in sports for a period of time can have great results spiritually if we spend that time in intercession and prayer. You choose to put spiritual exercise before physical exercise. Paul said, "Bodily exercise profits a little, but godliness is profitable for all things" (1 Tim. 4:8, NKJV).
- Give up pleasure reading. There are things we must read for our job, to prepare a Sunday school lesson or for other obligations. However, there are things we read in our spare time for relaxation and enjoyment. This can be reading a novel, the newspaper, a magazine, or material from the Internet. For a limited time, set aside reading and spend time in prayer.
- Restrict smartphone use and text messaging. While using high-tech communications may be necessary at times, they are also serious timewasters. When you give them up during a fast, spend the time in prayer. Time spent in the presence of God is better than time chatting with friends or playing with apps and games.
- Give up music. You may want to restrict pleasure music, listening only to Christian music while fasting. You can use Christian music for praise, worship and meditation. But eliminate secular music that takes your mind off Christ.

4. The John Wesley Fast

This is a fast that was practiced by John Wesley, the founder of Methodism, leading up to the monthly ministerial conference where pastors gathered for revival. For 10 days, John Wesley and other leaders ate bread (whole grains) and drank water as they prayed and prepared sermons to preach to the preachers. This type of fast is especially effective for preparing for ministry.

The ministers in the early Methodist church were not well trained; almost none had college or seminary education. They were called "plow-boy" preachers or "shop-keep" preachers. Most Methodist preachers had not prepared academically for ministry, but when they felt called of God they obeyed, leaving their trades to preach the gospel. The early Methodist church was more concerned about spiritual power than it was about ecclesiastical formats.

Most of these ministers were circuit-riding preachers who went out on horseback for 24 to 26 days at a time. Most looked after 20 to 40 local congregations. They usually preached the same sermon over and over to every church on their circuit. Then they gathered with the other circuit preachers to receive a fresh word from the Lord. John Wesley gathered leaders such as Francis Asbury, George Whitfield, Joe Parker and Charles Wesley to teach and instruct them. The leaders would preach one sermon after another and the circuit preachers would take copious notes, writing down everything they heard. When the conference was over, the circuit riders were refreshed and had new material to continue their preaching ministry to dozens of churches.

Wesley and the other Methodist leaders made a habit of fasting for 10 days before these monthly conferences. They knew that the word they brought to the circuit riders would be passed on to hundreds, if not thousands, of others—so it was of paramount importance to make sure every sermon was birthed in fasting and prayer. This grounding in spiritual discipline led to explosive growth in the early Methodist church. When the Revolutionary War began in 1775, there were 243 Methodist churches in the United States. By the war of 1812, there were more than 5,000. Fasting leaders produce growing churches.

5. The Rotational or Mayo Clinic Fast

This is primarily a medical fast to determine causes of sickness or other physical ailment. The patient begins with an absolute fast, not eating anything for 24 hours. This is to cleanse the systems of the body. Each following day (or sometimes longer) he eats from only one of the food groups. In this way, doctors attempt to isolate the causes of physical problems associated with particular foods.

There is little spiritual reason to choose the rotational fast over one of the other types, but if you are prescribed this type of fast by your doctor you can undertake it as a spiritual exercise as well as a medical necessity. It would certainly be a good time to pray for God's healing touch!

6. The Supernatural Fast

There are a few descriptions in Scripture of fasts that extended far past the point at which someone would die had not God sustained them supernaturally. Jesus wandered in the desert for 40 days, during which He ate no food (see Matt. 4:1-11). He may have drunk spring water or juice from desert cacti; Scripture does not say. Elijah traveled for 40 days to Mount Horeb without eating, after a meal provided by an angel of the Lord (see 1 Kings 19:1-8). Moses fasted for 40 days, neither eating nor drinking any liquid (see Exod. 34:28). While this is commendable, it is also supernatural. No one can survive 40 days without water. God did the miraculous in Moses' case.

Should you follow Moses' 40-day fast from both food and water, believing God will do the same for you? No! God is too good to tell us to do anything that would hurt our bodies. He wants us to care for our bodies, to honor Him through our bodies (see

1 Cor. 6:13-20). As I wrote in the introduction to this chapter, many stories in the Bible are descriptive. They describe what people did, including not drinking water for 40 days. But not all Bible stories are prescriptive, that is, a command for us to follow their example. As we read Scripture together, we must use discernment under the Holy Spirit's guidance to identify descriptive and prescriptive stories and to avoid confusing the two.

In a very real sense, every fast is supernatural. We are trusting God to sustain us and to answer our prayers—both supernatural activities! In order to honor God by taking responsible care of the bodies He has given us, we should avoid absolute fasts longer than three days, even as we recognize our God is able to do the miraculous. As Jesus said to His tempter, Satan: "It is also written: 'Do not put the Lord your God to the test'" (Matt. 4:7). Let's fast in such a way that we demonstrate our faith in God without testing Him.

THE BIBLICAL PURPOSES FOR FASTING

Isaiah 58 gives purposes for genuine biblical fasting. Rightly used, these purposes for fasting can help you touch God for those things for which you pray. Notice the purpose God gives for fasting. Following are seven purposes for fasting that are given in this Scripture.

"Is not this the fast that I have chosen? to loose the bands of wickedness, to undo the heavy burdens, and to let the oppressed go free, and that ye break every yoke? Is it not to deal thy bread to the hungry, and that thou bring the poor that are cast out to thy house? when thou seest the naked, that thou cover him; and that thou hide not thyself from thine own flesh? Then shall thy light break forth as the morning, and thine health shall spring forth speedily: and

thy righteousness shall go before thee; the glory of the Lord shall be thy reward" (vss. 6-8, KJV).

THE PURPOSE OF FASTING

- To loosen the bonds of wickedness, i.e. break addiction (**The Apostle's Fast**),

- To undo heavy burdens, i.e. to solve problems (**The Ezra Fast**),

- To let the oppressed, go free, i.e. revival and evangelism (**The Samuel Fast**),

- To allow light to break forth like the morning, i.e. guidance or direction (**The St. Paul Fast**),

- To cause health to spring forth speedily, i.e. for healing (**The Daniel Fast**),

- To cause the glory of the Lord to be their reward (or "rear guard," NIV), i.e., for protection from evil (**The Esther Fast**).

The following seven fasts are not the only methods of fasting available to the believer, nor are they totally separate from each other. Nor do they suggest that any one fast is only way to fast for these particular problems. These suggested fasts are models to use and should be adjusted to your own particular needs and desires as you seek to grow closer to God.

The Disciple's Fast from Addiction and Habits

Purpose: "To loose the bands of wickedness" (Isa. 58:6, KJV)—freeing yourself and others from addictions to sin.

Key Verse: "This kind goeth not out but by prayer and fasting" (Matt. 17:21, KJV).

Background: Jesus cast out a demon from a boy whom the disciples had failed to help.

Apparently, they had not taken seriously enough the way Satan had his claws set in the youth. The implication is that Jesus' disciples could have performed this exorcism had they been willing to undergo the discipline of fasting. Modern disciples also often make light of "besetting sins" we could cast out if we were serious enough to take part in such self-denying practices as fasting—hence the term "Disciple's Fast."

Many Christians are helpless victims to a habit or "besetting sin" (Heb. 12:1). This is not your average sin of neglect or momentary lapse. This is not even the sin of rebellion where God says, "Thou shalt not," and the person says, "I will" in God's face. These habits or "besetting" sins are habitual sinful behavior or attitudes that victimizes you. A besetting sin or habit puts you into bondage.

When you are a victim of a habit or besetting sin, you do not clench your fist in the face of God and transgress His purpose; you are helpless and broken because of your sin. A habit or besetting sin makes you a slave and takes away your will. You cry out "I can't help myself!" as one person once said, "I am forced to play a game where I always lose, and I can't quit playing. I hate the game...I hate playing...I hate life."

The Disciple's Fast targets a person's addiction so they can enter freedom in Christ.

The Ezra Fast to Solve Problems

Purpose: To "undo the heavy burdens" (Isa. 58:6, NKJV), inviting the Holy Spirit's aid in lifting loads and overcoming problems that keep yourself and your loved ones from walking joyfully with the Lord.

Key Verse: "So we fasted and entreated our God for this, and he answered our prayer" (Ezra 8:23, NKJV).

Background: Ezra the priest was charged with restoring the Law of Moses among the Jews as they rebuilt the city of Jerusalem by permission of Artaxerxes, King of Persia, where God's people had been captive. Despite this permission, Israel's enemies opposed them. Burdened with embarrassment about having to ask the Persian king for an army to protect them, Ezra fasted and prayed for an answer to his problem.

Everyone has problems and hard times. Job, in the oldest book of the Bible said, "Man who is born of woman is of few days and full of trouble" (Job 14:1, NKJV). Because of the nature of the world, everything that is made will break. Every person eventually will get old and feeble. Every business will collapse if not attended. Houses must be painted, cars must be tuned up, fields must be replanted every spring, and everyone faces problems that must be solved. Again, Job understood this: "Man is born into trouble as surely as the sparks fly upward" (Job 5:7, NIV).

The Ezra Fast is for difficult problems. You fast for a problem so God will send an answer. The Ezra Fast is for those who can't solve a problem, so now they fast and pray for an answer from God.

The Samuel Fast for Revival and Success for Ministry

Purpose: "To let the oppressed (physically and spiritually) go free" (Isa. 58:6 KJV)—to identify with enslaved people everywhere and to pray for God to bring people out of the kingdom of darkness into light.

Key Verse: "So they gathered together at Mizpah, drew water, and poured it out before the LORD. And they fasted that day, and said there, 'We have sinned against the LORD'" (I Sam. 7:6, NKJV).

Background: Samuel led God's people in a fast to celebrate the return of the ark of the covenant from its captivity by the Philistines. As a result of their fast, God sent revival to Israel.

The Samuel Fast for ministry and revival has been applied throughout church history. Before Jonathan Edwards preached his famous sermon, "Sinners in the Hands of An Angry God," he spent the previous 24 hours in an absolute fast. Many credit this sermon as the beginning of the first Great Awakening that shook America and England.

The Saint Paul's Fast for Guidance

Purpose: To allow God's "light (to) break forth like the morning" (Isa. 58:8, NKJV), bringing clearer perspective and insight as we make crucial decisions.

Key Verse: "And he (Saul, or Paul) was three days without sight, and neither ate nor drank" (Acts 9:9, NKJV).

Background: Saul of Tarsus, who became known as Paul after his conversion to Christ, was struck blind by the Lord in the act of persecuting Christians. He not only was without literal sight; he had no clue about what direction his life was to take. After going without food and praying three days, Paul was given both his eyesight and a spiritual vision for the future.

Everyone faces major decisions at some time in their life, so all will need the St. Paul Fast at some time. Major decisions redirect your entire life and even your destiny. These are decisions about what person to marry, accepting a new job or making a major change in life. These decisions can make or break you. And in many other ways you stand at a fork in the road and must make the decision to turn either to the left or the right.

If you knew everything that lay ahead on down the road, the decision would probably be easy. If you knew the good things that would happen, the decision would be easier. If you knew the dangers ahead, you might be discouraged. But you don't know, either way.

If you follow the St. Paul Fast, God will cause His "Light (to) break forth like the morning." This implies that when you focus on God's will instead of your own when you face such major decisions, He will bring you a clearer perspective and the insight you need to make crucial decisions.

The Daniel Fast for Health and Healing

Purpose: So "thine health shall spring forth" (Isa. 58:8, KJV).

Key Verse: "Daniel purposed in his heart that he would not defile himself with the portion of the king's delicacies, nor with the wine which he drank" (Dan. 1:8, NKJV).

Background: Daniel and his three fellow Hebrew captives kept themselves from pagan foods and became healthier than others in the king's court. Today, God can heal in response to prayer and fasting. Sometimes healing comes from an improved diet, and at other times God heals supernaturally.

God heals in many different ways. He heals when a disease or infection is stopped or reversed. He heals by a physician's correct diagnosis and prescription and application of medication, or by surgery that removes the cause of the illness, or by a change in the patient's physical routine. God can heal by supernatural intervention or by divine providence where He works His will by directing the circumstances of life.

Fasting plays many roles in healing. God heals supernaturally in response to a fast. Fasting also leads to God's guidance thorough circumstances so that the sick person adjusts his life to find healing. Then, too, fasting may result in a vow for a healthy lifestyle, as one vows a lifelong abstinence from alcoholic beverages, or other "risky" food habits that are not necessarily healthy. The person finds health from his vow.

The Esther Fast for Protection from the Evil One

Purpose: That "the glory of the Lord" will protect us from the Evil One.

Key Verses: "Fast for me...(and) my maids and I will fast...(and) I will go to the king...(and) she found favor in his sight" (Esther 4:16, 5:2, NKJV).

Background: Queen Esther, a Jewess in a pagan court, risked her life to save her people from threatened destruction by Ahasuerus (Xerxes), King of Persia. Before appearing before the king to petition him to save the Jews, Esther, her attendants, and her uncle Mordecai all fasted in order to appeal to God for His protection. Today, the Esther Fast will protect you from the danger of evil and satanic influences.

WHICH FAST IS RIGHT FOR YOU?

You may try various types of fasts at different times for different purposes. And that's great! The point of this chapter is there's no single "right" way to fast.

As you consider various ways of fasting, pray for the Spirit's guidance in choosing the right type for you and your circumstances. Talk to your doctor if you have medical concerns about withholding food and talk with your pastor or other spiritual mentor if you are uncertain which fasting method is best for you.

Once you have decided what type of fast to undertake, you are ready to complete your checklist and launch your fast (see chapter 1).

As you fill out your Fasting Checklist, there are six attitude preparations that will help you accomplish your faith goal. These are:

1. *Focus on your need.* You are going to do something that is not in your normal routine or inclination. You are choosing to not eat (or not participate in other activities) for a purpose. Focus on what you want God to do for you. Write the need exactly; it will help you focus what you are doing in your mind and bring out your sincerity to follow through.

2. *Focus on what you will do.* You are going to do something about the need. You are going to bring the problem to the Lord God of the universe. Focus on your prayer relationship with God to solve the problem.

3. *Begin and end with a purpose.* Some people find they have missed a meal and decide to call it a "fast." Just missing a meal because of circumstances is not a fast unless you purposed beforehand to pray and use the time of not eating for a spiritual purpose. God knows your heart. Also, don't enter into a fast with the idea of seeing how far you can go or how far you can hold out before you have to eat. Begin with purpose and end at the assigned time. Then begin on a specific date and end on a specific date. Finish strong! Then break your fast and eat in victory, with rejoicing.

4. *Gather the needed resources.* Before you begin your fast, gather resources that will be needed during the fast. If you're fasting for a person, get a picture of that person to hold during prayer and to heighten your memory. If you're fasting over bills, spread them out before you as you pray over them. Do the same if you're fasting about hiring or firing someone. Spread out the person's personnel records before you as you pray. Sometimes I select a spiritual book I want to read while fasting. Or it

could be some DVD that I want to see or a CD
that I want to hear.

5. *Remember the "inner journey principle."* Just as a
   person never takes a journey without first planning the journey within, so you must prepare
   yourself inwardly for a fast before you can be
   successful outwardly. In the same way that inner
   rings on a tree trunk tell of its growth, you will
   develop inner character as you control your outward diet.

6. *Make a vow.* Again, remember that fasting is a
   private vow that you make to God. Even if you
   are joining with others in your church in doing
   the fast (or even joining just one other person,
   such as your spouse), you must deal with the issue
   privately with God before you join with others.

Chapter 3

FASTING TO FIND HIS PRESENCE

I was invited by Ed Silvoso of Harvest Evangelism: Winning Cities to Christ, to fly to Mar del Plata, Argentina, to speak to approximately 14,000 pastors on the topic of fasting. When I walked into the basketball arena and saw the crowd, Ed apologized, "We only have 10,000 here today, but in my estimation, it looks more like 8,000." I was not discouraged by speaking to a smaller number, that crowd was one of the largest gatherings of Pentecostal preachers I had ever addressed.

As I took my seat, a well-dressed lady came to sit next to me. She spoke cultured English and explained that she was a Supreme Court justice in Argentina and had translated for meetings of the World Bank and the International Monetary Fund. She explained that she was a believer and heard that I was speaking. Then she said,

"God told me to come today and interpret for you…would you permit it?"

"Absolutely . . ." I explained that she was a gift of God and I needed her help.

GOD CHANGED MY SERMON

It was then that Ed Silvoso reached over, tapped me on the knee and said,

"God spoke to me this morning about your message . . ." Then he explained, "You should not preach on fasting today, but you must speak on knowing God intimately."

I panicked! Immediately my mind raced through the catalogue of sermons I could preach by heart. I did not have a sermon on the intimacy of God. I wanted to appeal to Ed that he was wrong! I had fasted repeatedly over this sermon on fasting…three or four times for perhaps 30 days. But then again, I knew I had to listen to the voice of God in my heart, as well as the voice of God speaking through other people. In my panic I was thinking,

What'll I do...?

Then I heard my name announced, and the audience began applauding. As my interpreter and I approached the podium, I was more surrendered to God than any time in my past. I was scared of embarrassing myself. My mind was empty. I was prepared to speak on fasting...but Ed had said, "God spoke to me and you are to preach on knowing God intimately." Inwardly I prayed again,

Jesus, help me!

I cannot preach bombastically like Pentecostal preachers. So, God sent a quiet dignified woman to help me, one who could speak with authority; but more importantly, she could speak with clarity. I knew the audience would understand what I said; if I only knew what I was going to say.

Jesus, help me! I prayed over and over until a thought came to me. I remembered something I had written in an article on *knowing God intimately* a couple of weeks earlier. I began to tell the 8,000 people waiting what I remembered.

CLOSE TO GOD
AS THE ANGELS

If you are going to become intimate with God, you must get close to God. And no one has ever been closer to God than the two angels on the lid of the Ark of the Covenant. "You shall make a mercy seat of pure gold; two and a half cubits *shall be* its length and a cubit and a half its width. And you shall make two cherubim of gold; of hammered work you shall make them at the two ends of the mercy seat" (Ex. 25:17-18, NKJV).

I explained the Ark was about the size of a chest and its lid was called the mercy seat. God came down to earth to sit on a box (the word Ark means box), and the lid of the box was a solid gold mercy seat. Located on the right and left of the mercy seat were two angels made of pure gold.

PURE GOLD
SUGGESTS HOLINESS

The two angels weren't just made of gold but of *pure* gold. Gold has several degrees of purity, and 24-karat gold was the purest. Doesn't everyone know that the most expensive gold is the purest? God told Moses to make the angels of pure gold, because God wants purity in the lives of those who worship Him and are close to Him.

The difference between pure gold and a lesser grade of gold is *fire.* And the hotter the purifying fire, the more dross and impurities are burned away. As the fire is heated, the gold melts and the sludge floats to the top where it is skimmed away, leaving refined gold.

Because God wants those closest to Him to be holy, He adds the fire of suffering and difficulties of life to the intercessors to rid them of their impurities. And those who are closest to Him get the most attention. Sometimes He allows financial reverses to strike devoted believers so they will go immediately to Him in prayer.

Because of financial disasters in Argentina, its people had cried out honestly to God in prayer. And while they are crying to God and seeking His presence, they are releasing their covetous grip on material possessions. Fire burns away the impurity of their greed.

Do you have any impurities that need to be burned away? Do you feel fire licking around the edges of an unyielding possession? Don't complain to God, or doubt Him. Don't think that He doesn't love you. Instead, let your prayer be, "O God, do Your work in my life!" Let His purifying fire upgrade you into pure gold.

When gold is first put into the goldsmith's fire, the heat burns away the dirtiest impurities, including trash and filth. The same process happens in the Christian life. God first touches our fleshly sins, our sexual sins, and our outward problems.

The goldsmith turns up the flame so the fire can burn away unseen impurities. Again, the same thing happens in the life of the believer. After you've been separated from outward sins, God then focuses on inward sins that hinder your walk with Him. The fire of conviction burns away unseen impurities of attitude and desires, little things you allow to block your communion with God.

So why did God demand that the angels and the mercy seat be made of pure gold? Because God Himself is sitting with them right there on the mercy seat. Since He is a pure God, He would not sit there if the mercy seat and the angels were made of impure gold.

How pure is pure gold, and how does the goldsmith know the gold is pure? You can't tell how pure the gold is just by looking at it. Pureness is not determined by how long you leave gold in the fire or how big the flames are. Only when all dross is gone is the gold pure; and the goldsmith will know when the gold is at that pure stage only by looking into the golden liquid as he would look into a mirror, to see his face. When he sees himself in the gold, then he knows the gold is pure.

Likewise, when God looks into your soul and sees Himself, then He knows you are pure gold. Why does God allow the flames of trials in your life? He's burning away dross, so He can see Himself in your life.

Today, who does God see when He looks into your heart? You—or Himself?

ANGELS WERE SCULPTURED

The two worshiping angels were sculptured from one piece of gold—not poured into a mold but beaten into form. They were shaped and crafted by hand into the proper form. And the purer the gold, the easier it was to sculpture as the craftsman intended. "And thou shalt make two cherubims of gold, of beaten work shalt thou make them, in the two ends of the mercy seat" (Ex. 15:18, KJV).

This reminds us that worshipers are not formed easily or cheaply. They are literally shaped by God's hands into the worshiping position. To be beaten is not the same thing as to be purified. When you are pure, it means you have separated yourself from sin, i.e., you are holy. When you are sculptured—or beaten with hammers—you become yielded to God and His purpose for you.

We are also reminded that all things that are poured into the same mold become identical. But when you sculpture something, it is unique. A sculptor cannot beat two images into identical shape. Each is a little different from the other. So, as God forms us into worshipers, each of us is a little different from the other, although all of us are fashioned by the hands of the same Master Craftsman.

And don't forget that while cheap imitations can be made by pouring liquid into a mold, a genuine work of art is sculptured by a master craftsman. He puts his personality and talent into what he forms. So, God, the Master Craftsman, puts unique life, *His* life and design, into us, when He molds us into worshipers.

Can you see the goldsmith shaping a worshiping angel? Is a wing not lifted correctly in praise? A few touches from the Master's hand will bring it into the proper place. Perhaps the head is not bowed as it should be. A touch of the right tool, the right hammer, will correct the problem.

What kind of hammer does God use on you? He always has the right kind of tool to use on the unique problem of pride. He might use a different hammer on greed and an entirely different hammer on lust. Because my problems are different from yours, God will use a different hammer on me than on you. He has all kinds of hammers for all kinds of problems. He uses His tools on gold until each of us is just right—just right for worship.

If you won't allow the Lord to use His hammer on you, then something else or someone else will have to beat you into submission. If you are beaten by the world, the flesh and the devil, you can end up broken—in body and spirit—perhaps for your whole life. That's not God's plan. He doesn't beat you to crush you. No! God uses His hammer to mold you into a true worshiper. He doesn't want to break you but to bend your heart to His will, to enable you to look more like Him. "But we all, with unveiled face, beholding as in a mirror the glory of the Lord, are being transformed into the same image from glory to glory, just as by the Spirit of the Lord" (2 Cor. 3:18, NKJV).

The audience was still and reverent. No shouts of "AMEN," no shouts like I heard during the previous sermon. Like the silent morning fields waiting for the dawning of the glorious sun so they can break into the harvest, the Pentecostal pastors waited anxiously for the message God was revealing to their hearts.

SPREAD WINGS TO WORSHIP

The angels with outstretched wings remind us of worshipers stretching out their hands in praise to God. God consented to dwell at the mercy seat in the Tabernacle not just because Moses followed the blueprint to the letter of the Law, and not because of the expensive gold appointments. He dwelt there because the angel's outspread wings were praising Him. The Lord came down to live in the praises of Israel (see Ps. 22:3).

So, the angels on the Ark of the Covenant remind us of the importance of worship. Before you ask for something, make sure you worship the Lord first, so He will come to you with His presence.

THE ANGELS GAZED ON GOD

There is another thing about the angels who are close to God. "And the cherubim shall stretch out *their* wings above, covering the mercy seat with their wings, and they shall face one another; the faces of the cherubim *shall be* toward the mercy seat" Ex. 25:20, NKJV). Those closest to God want to gaze upon Him. Their first glance is not to the beauty of the Tabernacle, nor do they look to see the carvings throughout the interior. No! They look intimately to God.

Note their gaze was toward each other, but each was not looking at the other. No! Their gaze was upon God who sat between them. The top or lid of the Ark was the mercy seat. That's the place on earth where God sat. God promises, "And there I will meet with thee, and I will commune with thee" (Ex. 25:22, KJV).

You look at God in prayer, and you must be close to Him if you are to know Him intimately. How close to God are you today?

Your gaze must be constant. You must see God every morning the first thing upon arising. You must see God in all your activities each day, all day. You must gaze upon God in prayer before you go to sleep at night.

Next, I described the wings of the angels stretched out in worship to God. "The cherubims shall stretch forth their wings on high, covering the mercy seat with their wings" (Ex. 25:20, KJV).

I said to the pastors, "When you get close to God, you lift your hands in worship to God. Your outward body reflects your inner soul. You give praise to God with your hands."

Hands were lifted heavenward all over the audience. The peoples' hearts were with me, 8,000 pastors and I were one. I had prayed frantically, *Jesus, help me!* He was doing it. My quiet presentation was having a quiet salutatory effect on the pastors, different than the previous loud shouts. Yet both responses glorified God, each in its own way.

I did not preach long, maybe 20-25 minutes. As I came to the conclusion, I began appealing for action.

"What shall we do?"

I repeated the question 2 or 3 times for emphasis, perhaps getting more bold or louder than I had preached throughout the sermon. I had just emphasized the angels' bowed heads and wings stretched out to God. So, I said dramatically,

"WE MUST FALL ON OUR FACE BEFORE GOD…"

They did! All over the arena they began dropping to the floor, lying in the aisle and on the floor beneath their benches. Some kneeling at their benches. Some sitting but bowed in reverential worship.

As I saw them dropping to the floor, a very unspiritual thought popped into my mind, *I didn't mean fall literally…* Yet at the same time, I realized it was a sacred moment. God was working in hearts.

Their prayers swelled into a great chorus of praise to God. He was receiving a concert of prayer. Throughout history, God's people have prayed in unison, all praying out loud at the same time. Whereas some may hear a loud noise of everyone speaking at the same time, God listens and enjoys the concert of praise from the hearts of His people as one might enjoy a symphony, each instrument playing a different note at its appointed time, but blending in perfect harmony.

HOW TO FAST TO KNOW GOD INTIMATELY

1. **Intimacy begins with God's invitation to come to Him.** We are invited to come to God to both know Him and His power. "Come, behold the works of the LORD" (Ps. 46:8; 66:5). And how do you respond when someone calls you to come to them? It begins with a listening ear; we listen to God's voice in His Word. Then we turn our attention to the one calling to us; we focus our attention on God. We focus to find out where the voice is located. Since God is everywhere at the same time, we can come to Him from anyplace, at any time. But we also know there are certain places we experience God best, so we come to those places. Sometimes it's in a church, sometimes in our homes at Bible study, or in our prayer closet.

   Jesus has invited us, "Come to Me, all *you* who labor and are heavy laden, and I will give you rest" (Matt. 11:28, NKJV). This is His call to bring our sins or problems to Him.

   Jesus also calls us to service, "Come ye after me, and I will make you to become fishers of men"

(Mark 1:17, KJV). So, whether we need intimacy in service, victory over sin, or worship intimacy, we must begin our search for intimacy by coming to God.

2. **<u>God invites us to know Him.</u>** God wants intimacy with us for He invites, "Be still, and know that I am God" (Ps. 46:10). Intimacy begins when we stop what we are doing and think so we can "be still." That means we come to an end of ourselves. It's then that we can begin to find the presence of God.

We can know God because He is knowable. We are made in His image, and because He thinks, we are rational. Because God has the emotions to love the sinner but hate the sin, so we have emotions to love God's mercy and fear God's wrath. Because God knows Himself, and we are made in His image, we can know Him.

We are commanded to know God in comparison to knowing our humanity. "Know that the Lord, He *is* God; *It is* He *who* has made us" (Ps. 100:3, NKJV). Therefore, God understands the vast gap between Him and us.

God knows Himself perfectly because God is perfect in all things. But we can only know Him partially because we are limited humans. Even though we can never perfectly know all things about God, we can know more today than we knew yesterday. We can grow in our understanding of God. That means today I can be closer and more intimate with God than I was yesterday.

3. **<u>Intimacy is experienced in God's atmospheric presence.</u>** I can make a motel room a sanctuary. Sometimes I travel to speak, and I get to my motel room late. The next morning I'm tired when I pray or I'm not wide awake, and my prayers seem to bounce off the walls or go no further than the ceiling. It's at that moment of frustration that I remember the supernatural power of worship. Jesus told us, "The Father is seeking worship" (John 4:23, ELT). That means God goes to where people worship Him to receive their worship.

In the movie, *Field of Dreams*, the Iowa farmer heard the phrase, "If you build it, they will come." So apply this insight to seeking God's intimacy, "If you worship the Father, He will come to receive it."

Therefore, when I pray and feel I'm not getting through to God, I begin worshiping Him with His many names. It's then I feel His presence. Note the phrase, "I feel His presence." He was always there, but worship changes me and equips me to experience God's presence.

I call this God's atmospheric presence. Just as I can feel moisture in the air when it's not raining, so I can feel God's presence with me when I pray and worship. Also, sometimes we walk into a church service and feel the presence of God among the people. This is in stark contrast to the empty or dead feeling we feel in some other church services.

WRAP-UP

Your soul can embrace God as your spiritual eyes focus on God. As a result, you will understand God and His will for your life as you see Him because of your fast.

Your soul's spiritual ears can hear God, so you can know His voice and understand what He wants you to know. Fasting can turn your attention to God to know what He wants you to learn.

Your spiritual fingers can touch God so that you feel His presence when you pray and He's there when you reach out to Him. Fasting will give you assurance of your relationship with God.

Your spiritual nostrils can sense the beauty of God's perfume as you can smell the aroma of His spiritual food.

Your spiritual taste can be satisfied as you rest in God's presence. Just as food pleases the taste and strengthens the body, so your spiritual taste can bring satisfaction to your life and strength to your soul.

When your life touches God, surrender to His divine purpose. Reach out and touch God right now, and you will find Him reaching out to you.

Sincerely yours in Christ

Elmer Towns

PART TWO

21 DAYS OF PRAYER AND FASTING

LESSONS

THREE LESSONS

THESE can be communicated to those who will join you in the 21 days of prayer and fasting.

There are three lessons plans for each of your followers who will join you in fasting. Each lesson includes teacher outline, listener's outline and PowerPoint to help you communicate the sermon/lesson to your followers.

Lesson 1: What Fasting Is and How to Get Started

Lesson 2: How to Go About Fasting

Lesson 3: Fasting to Know God Intimately

Lesson 1:

WHAT FASTING IS AND HOW TO GET STARTED

A. CHRISTIAN FASTING IS A NON-REQUIRED DISCIPLINE

Jesus said, "When you fast" (Matt. 6:16). Did Jesus mean you must fast, or did He give you an option? "If you fast?" Christian fasting:

1. **Alters** your diet, or

2. **Eliminates** food and/or drink

3. For a **biblical purpose**,

4. Accompanied with **prayer**.

B. RICHARD FOSTER SAID THERE HAS NOT BEEN A SIGNIFICANT WORK ON FASTING IN 100 YEARS. WHY?

1. **Boomers**.

2. **Addiction / food**.

3. **No revival**.

4. **Need discipline and character**.

5. Abundance of food has **isolated us from realities of hunger**.

6. Not **healthier**.

7. No **testimony**.

8. Growth of **demonic forces**.

C. HOW TO BEGIN FASTING

1. Ask God to **lead you** in your fast. Jesus describes fasting in the context of the Lord's Prayer in Matthew. 6:9-15. "When ye fast, be not...of a sad countenance...but anoint thy head, and wash thy face, that thou appear not unto men to fast" (Matt. 6:16-18, KJV).

   a. **Private** for a personal request.

   b. **Joint** for a group project.

2. Write out your **purpose, plan and length**.

3. Begin with a **one-day fast**, i.e., the (Yom Kippur) Day of Atonement Fast. "On the tenth day of the seventh month of each year, you must go without eating to show sorrow for your sins" (Lev. 16:29, CEV). The Yom Kippur Fast is from sundown to sundown (Jewish day).

   a. If the issue is greater than a one-day fast; try fasting **one day a week** for 3 weeks or 7 weeks.

   b. Better to take small steps and **succeed**, than a giant step and **fail**.

4. **Eat a light snack** before sundown (English high tea).

5. Dedicate time for meals **to prayer**.

6. Bring Bible, books, notes, etc., (see specific fast).

D. VARIOUS KINDS OF FASTS

1. One-day fast — a **Yom Kippur** fast.

2. Three-day fast – **Esther** fast

3. Ten-day fast – Daniel

4. Twenty-one day fast – **Daniel**

5. Fasting from sweets and deserts

6. The Daniel Fast – eating only **vegetables**, no meat, sweets, etc.

7. Fasting from coffee, stimulants etc.

8. Give up sports, hobbies, i.e., golf, tennis, etc.

9. Give up television, newspaper, etc.

10. Your fast: ____.

When things and events are given up, spend this extra time in prayer, Bible reading, etc.

E. PRACTICAL HELP TO BEGIN

General Checklist

Purpose:

____

Fast: What you will withhold

____

Begin: Date _____________________________ Time _____________________

End: Date _______________________________ Time _____________________

Vow: I believe God is the only answer to my request and that prayer without fasting is not enough to get an answer to my need. Therefore, by faith I am fasting because I need God to work in this matter.

Bible Basis: My Bible promise

____

____

Resources: What I need during this fast

____

____

With God being my strength and grace being my basis, I commit myself to the above fast.

____
Signed   Date

Lesson 1:

WHAT FASTING IS AND HOW TO GET STARTED

A. CHRISTIAN FASTING IS A NON-REQUIRED DISCIPLINE

Jesus said, "When you fast" (Matt. 6:16). Did Jesus mean you must fast, or did He give you an option? "If you fast?" Christian fasting:

1. __________ your diet, or

2. __________ food and/or drink

3. For a __________ ,

4. Accompanied with __________ .

B. RICHARD FOSTER SAID THERE HAS NOT BEEN A SIGNIFICANT WORK ON FASTING IN 100 YEARS. WHY?

1. ___________________ .

2. ___________________ .

3. ___________________ .

4. ___________________ .

5. Abundance of food has ___________________________________ .

6. Not ___________________ .

7. No ___________________ .

8. Growth of ___________________ .

C. HOW TO BEGIN FASTING

1. Ask God to ___________ in your fast. Jesus describes fasting in the context of the Lord's Prayer in Matthew 6:9-15. "When ye fast, be not...of a sad countenance...but anoint thy head, and wash thy face, that thou appear not unto men to fast" (Matt. 6:16-18, KJV).

   a. ___________ for a personal request.

   b. ___________ for a group project.

2. Write out your ___________________ .

3. Begin with a ___________________, i.e., the (Yom Kippur) Day of Atonement Fast. "On the tenth day of the seventh month of each year, you must go without eating to show sorrow for your sins" (Lev. 16:29, CEV). The Yom Kippur Fast is from sundown to sundown (Jewish day).

   a. If the issue is greater than a one-day fast; try fasting ___________________ for 3 weeks or 7 weeks.

   b. Better to take small steps and ___________, than a giant step and ___________ .

4. ___________________ before sundown (English high tea).

5. Dedicate time for meals ___________ .

6. Bring Bible, books, notes, etc., (see specific fast).

D. VARIOUS KINDS OF FASTS

1. One-day fast — a _____________________ fast.

2. Three-day fast – _____________________ fast

3. Ten-day fast – Daniel

4. Twenty-one day fast – _____________________

5. Fasting from sweets and deserts

6. The Daniel Fast – eating only _____________________, no meat, sweets, etc.

7. Fasting from coffee, stimulants etc.

8. Give up sports, hobbies, i.e., golf, tennis, etc.

9. Give up television, newspaper, etc.

10. Your fast: _____________________________________.

When things and events are given up, spend this extra time in prayer, Bible reading, etc.

E. PRACTICAL HELP TO BEGIN

General Checklist

Purpose:

____

Fast: What you will withhold

____

Begin: Date _____________________ Time _____________________

End: Date _____________________ Time _____________________

Vow: I believe God is the only answer to my request and that prayer without fasting is not enough to get an answer to my need. Therefore, by faith I am fasting because I need God to work in this matter.

Bible Basis: My Bible promise

____

____

Resources: What I need during this fast

____

____

With God being my strength and grace being my basis, I commit myself to the above fast.

____

Signed   Date

Lesson 2:

HOW TO GO ABOUT FASTING

A. WHAT IS FASTING?

1. Christian fasting is a non-required **discipline** that:

    a. **Alters** your diet,

    b. **Eliminates** food and/or drink,

    c. For a **biblical purpose**,

    d. Accompanied with **prayer**.

B. KINDS OF FASTS

1. The **Normal** fast is going without food for a certain period of time, drinking only liquid (water and/or juice).

2. The **Absolute** fast, no water or food at all. Should be short.

3. The **Partial** fast, omitting certain foods on a schedule of limited eating, i.e., only one meal a day, only vegetables, etc.

4. The **Wesley** fast is eating only bread (whole grains) and water.

5. The **Rotation** fast is eating or omitting certain families of food for a designated time. Some food is eaten every day. The Mayo Clinic fast is eating only one food group a day, omitting the other food groups, used as medical research to determine reaction (allergies) to a particular food group.

6. The **Supernatural** fast.

C. THE NINE FASTS IN SCRIPTURES

"Is this not the fast that I have chosen: to loose the bonds of wickedness, to undo the heavy burdens, to let the oppressed go free, and that you break every yoke? Is it not to share your bread with the hungry, and that you bring to your house the poor who are cast out; when you see the naked, that you cover him, and not hide yourself from your own flesh? Then your light shall break forth like the morning, your healing shall spring forth speedily, and your righteousness shall go before you; the glory of the Lord shall be your rear guard" (Isaiah 58:6-8, NKJV).

D. WHAT FASTS ACCOMPLISH

1. The Apostle's Fast:

   - Issue: To free oneself from **addiction to sin**.

   - Verse: "This kind goeth not out but by prayer and fasting" (Matthew 17:21, KJV).

2. The Ezra Fast:

   - Issue: To solve **problems**.

   - Verse: "So we fasted and entreated our God for this, and He answered our prayer" (Ezra 8:23, NKJV).

3. The Samuel Fast:

   - Issue: To bring **evangelism and revival**.

   - Verse: "So they gathered together at Mizpah, drew water, and poured it out before the Lord. And they fasted that day" (1 Samuel 7:6, NKJV).

4. The Elijah Fast:

   - Issue: To solve **emotional and mental problems**.

   - Verse: "He (Elijah)...went in the strength of that food forty days" (1 Kings 19:8).

5. The Widow's Fast:

   - Issue: To provide for **physical needs of others**.

   - Verse: "Is it (the fast) not to share your bread with the hungry?" (Isaiah 58:7, NKJV).

6. The Saint Paul Fast:

   - Issue: To make **life-changing decisions**.

   - Verse: "He was three days without sight, and neither ate nor drank" (Acts 9:9, NKJV).

7. The Daniel Fast:

   - Issue: For physical **health or healing**.

   - Verse: "Test your servants ten days...give us vegetables to eat and water to drink" (Daniel 1:12, NKJV).

8. The John the Baptist Fast:

   - Issue: For your **testimony**.

   - Verse: "He will be great in the sight of the Lord, and shall drink neither wine nor strong drink" (Luke 1:15, NKJV).

9. The Esther Fast:

   - Issue: For **protection from the evil one**.

   - Verse: "Gather all the Jews...fast for me; neither eat nor drink for three days, night or day. My maiden and I will fast likewise" (Esther 4:16, NKJV).

Lesson 2:

HOW TO GO ABOUT FASTING

A. WHAT IS FASTING?

1. Christian fasting is a non-required ______________ that:

    a. ______________ your diet,

    b. ______________ food and/or drink,

    c. For a ______________________,

    d. Accompanied with ______________.

B. KINDS OF FASTS

1. The ______________ fast is going without food for a certain period of time, drinking only liquid (water and/or juice).

2. The ______________ fast, no water or food at all. Should be short.

3. The ______________ fast, omitting certain foods on a schedule of limited eating, i.e., only one meal a day, only vegetables, etc.

4. The ______________ fast is eating only bread (whole grains) and water.

5. The ______________ fast is eating or omitting certain families of food for a designated time. Some food is eaten every day. The Mayo Clinic fast is eating only one food group a day, omitting the other food groups, used as medical research to determine reaction (allergies) to a particular food group.

6. The ______________ fast.

C. THE NINE FASTS IN SCRIPTURES

"Is this not the fast that I have chosen: to loose the bonds of wickedness, to undo the heavy burdens, to let the oppressed go free, and that you break every yoke? Is it not to share your bread with the hungry, and that you bring to your house the poor who are cast out; when you see the naked, that you cover him, and not hide yourself from your own flesh? Then your light shall break forth like the morning, your healing shall spring forth speedily, and your righteousness shall go before you; the glory of the Lord shall be your rear guard" (Isaiah 58:6-8, NKJV).

D. WHAT FASTS ACCOMPLISH

1. The Apostle's Fast:

   - Issue: To free oneself from ___________________.

   - Verse: "This kind goeth not out but by prayer and fasting" (Matthew 17:21, KJV).

2. The Ezra Fast:

   - Issue: To solve ___________________.

   - Verse: "So we fasted and entreated our God for this, and He answered our prayer" (Ezra 8:23, NKJV).

3. The Samuel Fast:

   - Issue: To bring ___________________.

   - Verse: "So they gathered together at Mizpah, drew water, and poured it out before the Lord. And they fasted that day" (1 Samuel 7:6, NKJV).

4. The Elijah Fast:

   - Issue: To solve ___________________.

   - Verse: "He (Elijah)...went in the strength of that food forty days" (1 Kings 19:8, NKJV).

5. The Widow's Fast:

   - Issue: To provide for ___________________.

   - Verse: "Is it (the fast) not to share your bread with the hungry?" (Isaiah 58:7, NKJV).

6. The Saint Paul Fast:

- Issue: To make _____________________.

- Verse: "He was three days without sight, and neither ate nor drank" (Acts 9:9, NKJV).

7. The Daniel Fast:

- Issue: For physical _____________________.

- Verse: "Test your servants ten days...give us vegetables to eat and water to drink" (Daniel 1:12, NKJV).

8. The John the Baptist Fast:

- Issue: For your ___________.

- Verse: "He will be great in the sight of the Lord, and shall drink neither wine nor strong drink" (Luke 1:15, NKJV).

9. The Esther Fast:

- Issue: For _______________________________.

- Verse: "Gather all the Jews...fast for me; neither eat nor drink for three days, night or day. My maiden and I will fast likewise" (Esther 4:16, NKJV).

Lesson 3:

FASTING TO KNOW GOD INTIMATELY

A. GOD TOUCHED 8,000 PENTECOSTAL PREACHERS

1. Ed Silvoso of Harvest Evangelism invited me to del Plata, Argentina, to speak to approximately 8,000 pastors, the largest gathering of Pentecostal preachers I had ever addressed.

2. The preacher before me **motivated** the crowd, there were shouts of "HALLELUJAH!" and "PRAISE THE LORD!"

3. Five men approached me. "We have read your book on fasting...and have come to pray for God to use you." They laid hands on me and **prayed quietly over me**.

4. A well-dressed lady who spoke cultured English, and was a Supreme Court justice in Argentina was a believer. She said, "God told me to **interpret** for you today. Would you permit it?"

5. A small elderly lady holding a basin and a bottle of water and a towel asked, "May I wash your feet to **prepare** you for ministry?"

6. "I must go to the platform immediately," I explained. "But I receive your blessing." God could see her heart and blessed my sermon.

7. Silvoso said, "God spoke to me this morning. You should not preach on fasting today, but you must speak on **knowing** God intimately."

8. Inwardly I prayed again, *Jesus, help me*!

9. I remembered something I had written just a couple of weeks earlier.

1. If you are going to become intimate with God, you must get close to God. And no one has ever been closer to God than the **two angels** on the lid of the Ark of the Covenant.

2. "You shall make a mercy seat of pure gold; two and a half cubits shall be its length and a cubit and a half its width. And you shall make two cherubim of gold; of hammered work you shall make them at the two ends of the mercy seat" (Exodus 25:17-18, NKJV).

3. The Ark was about the size of a **chest**, and its lid was called the mercy seat. God sat on a box, not a throne. The word *ark* means "box."

4. Located on the right and left sides were two angels sculptured of pure gold. Pure gold suggests holiness.

5. Gold has **several degrees** of purity, 24-karat gold being the purest.

6. The angels were pure gold, because God wants purity in the lives of those who **worship Him** and are **close to Him**.

7. The **difference** between pure gold and a lesser grade of gold is fire—and the hotter the purifying fire, the more dross and impurities are burned away.

8. Sludge floats to the top and is **skimmed away**, leaving refined gold.

9. God uses the fire of suffering and difficulties to rid us of **impurities**.

10. Sometimes God **allows** physical failures, financial reverse, or family difficulties.

11. Fire burns away the impurity of **greed and self, and other sins**.

12. First, God touches our **fleshly sins** and other outward problems.

13. Next, God focuses on any **inward sins** that hinder your walk with Him.

14. Why did God demand that the angels and the mercy seat be made of pure God? Because **He Himself** was going to sit there. God is pure, so He would not sit there if the mercy seat and the angels were made of impure gold.

15. How pure is pure gold? The goldsmith will know when he looks into a mirror of gold to see **his own face**.

1. Two worshiping angels were sculpted from a piece of gold—not poured into a mold but **beaten** into the proper form. "And thou shalt make two cherubims of gold, of beaten work shalt thou make them, in the two ends of the mercy seat" (Exodus 25:18, KJV).

2. The purer the gold, the easier it would be for the craftsman to **sculpt** them.

3. They are literally shaped by hand into the **worshiping position**.

4. When you are pure, you have separated yourself from sin, i.e., you are **holy**. When you are sculpted—or beaten with hammers—you become **yielded to God**.

5. Things that are poured into the same mold become identical, something sculpted is **unique**.

6. Each of us is a little different from the other. All of us are fashioned by the hands of the same **Master Craftsman**.

7. The sculptor puts his **personality and talent** into what he forms.

8. The Master Craftsman puts unique life—**His life**—and design into you when He shapes you into a worshiper.

9. What kind of **hammer** does God use on you? A different hammer on greed and an entirely different hammer on lust.

10. If you won't allow the **Lord** to use His hammer on you, then something else or someone else will have to beat you into submission.

11. God doesn't want to break you, but to **bend** your heart to His will. "But we all, with unveiled face, beholding as in a mirror the glory of the Lord, are being transformed into the same image from glory to glory, just as by the Spirit of the Lord" (2 Corinthians 3:18, NKJV).

D. SPREAD WINGS TO WORSHIP

1. The angels outstretched wings reminds us of worshipers stretching out their hands in **praise to God**.

2. God **dwelt** between the outstretched wings of the angels. The Lord came down to live in the praises of Israel (see Psalm 22:3).

3. Before you ask for something, make sure you worship the Lord first. Then He will come to you with His presence.

E. THE ANGELS GAZED ON GOD

1. "And the cherubim shall stretch out their wings above, covering the mercy seat with their wings, and they shall face one another; the faces of the cherubim shall be toward the mercy seat" (Exodus 25:20, NKJV). Those closest to God want to **gaze** upon Him.

2. Their gaze was toward each other, but each **was not** looking at the other. Their gaze was **upon** God.

3. On the top, or lid of the Ark, the **mercy seat** is the place on earth where God sat. "And there I will meet with thee, and I will commune with thee" (Exodus 25:22, KJV).

4. Prayer is how we look at God. We must be close to Him if we are to see Him **clearly** and know Him **intimately**.

F. ANGELS REACHING OUT TO GOD

1. "The cherubims shall stretch forth their wings on high, covering the mercy seat with their wings" (Exodus 25:20, KJV).

2. Your outward body reflects your **inner soul**. You give praise to God with your hands.

3. As I came to the conclusion, I asked the question, *"What shall we do?"*

4. I said, dramatically, *"WE MUST FALL ON OUR FACE BEFORE GOD!"* And they did!

FASTING TO KNOW GOD INTIMATELY

A. GOD TOUCHED 8,000 PENTECOSTAL PREACHERS

1. Ed Silvoso of Harvest Evangelism invited me to del Plata, Argentina, to speak to approximately 8,000 pastors, the largest gathering of Pentecostal preachers I had ever addressed.

2. The preacher before me ___________ the crowd, there were shouts of "HALLELUJAH!" and "PRAISE THE LORD!"

3. Five men approached me. "We have read your book on fasting...and have come to pray for God to use you." They laid hands on me and ___________________.

4. A well-dressed lady spoke who cultured English, and was a Supreme Court justice in Argentina was a believer. She said, "God told me to ___________ for you today. Would you permit it?"

5. A small elderly lady holding a basin and a bottle of water and a towel asked, "May I wash your feet to ___________ you for ministry?"

6. "I must go to the platform immediately," I explained. "But I receive your blessing." God could see her heart and blessed my sermon.

7. Silvoso said, "God spoke to me this morning. You should not preach on fasting today, but you must speak on ___________ God intimately."

8. Inwardly I prayed again, *Jesus, help me*!

9. I remembered something I had written just a couple of weeks earlier.

1. If you are going to become intimate with God, you must get close to God. And no one has ever been closer to God than the ___________________ on the lid of the Ark of the Covenant.

2. "You shall make a mercy seat of pure gold; two and a half cubits shall be its length and a cubit and a half its width. And you shall make two cherubim of gold; of hammered work you shall make them at the two ends of the mercy seat" (Exodus 25:17-18, NKJV).

3. The Ark was about the size of a __________, and its lid was called the mercy seat. God sat on a box, not a throne. The word *ark* means "box."

4. Located on the right and left sides were two angels sculptured of pure gold. Pure gold suggests holiness.

5. Gold has ___________________ of purity, 24-karat gold being the purest.

6. The angels were pure gold, because God wants purity in the lives of those who ___________________ and are ___________________.

7. The __________ between pure gold and a lesser grade of gold is fire—and the hotter the purifying fire, the more dross and impurities are burned away.

8. Sludge floats to the top and is ___________________, leaving refined gold.

9. God uses the fire of suffering and difficulties to rid us of __________.

10. Sometimes God __________ physical failures, financial reverse, or family difficulties.

11. Fire burns away the impurity of ____.

12. First, God touches our ___________________ and other outward problems.

13. Next, God focuses on any ___________________ that hinder your walk with Him.

14. Why did God demand that the angels and the mercy seat be made of pure God? Because ___________________ was going to sit there. God is pure, so He would not sit there if the mercy seat and the angels were made of impure gold.

15. How pure is pure gold? The goldsmith will know when he looks into a mirror of gold to see ___________________.

C. ANGELS WERE SCULPTED

1. Two worshiping angels were sculpted from a piece of gold—not poured into a mold but ______________ into the proper form. "And thou shalt make two cherubims of gold, of beaten work shalt thou make them, in the two ends of the mercy seat" (Exodus 25:18, KJV).

2. The purer the gold, the easier it would be for the craftsman to ______________ them.

3. They are literally shaped by hand into the ______________.

4. When you are pure, you have separated yourself from sin, i.e., you are ______________. When you are sculpted—or beaten with hammers—you become ______________.

5. Things that are poured into the same mold become identical, something sculpted is ______________.

6. Each of us is a little different from the other. All of us are fashioned by the hands of the same ______________.

7. The sculptor puts his ______________ into what he forms.

8. The Master Craftsman puts unique life— ______________ —and design into you when He shapes you into a worshiper.

9. What kind of ______________ does God use on you? A different hammer on greed and an entirely different hammer on lust.

10. If you won't allow the ______________ to use His hammer on you, then something else or someone else will have to beat you into submission.

11. God doesn't want to break you, but to ______________ your heart to His will. "But we all, with unveiled face, beholding as in a mirror the glory of the Lord, are being transformed into the same image from glory to glory, just as by the Spirit of the Lord" (2 Corinthians 3:18, NKJV).

D. SPREAD WINGS TO WORSHIP

1. The angels outstretched wings reminds us of worshipers stretching out their hands in

   ______________________.

2. God __________ between the outstretched wings of the angels. The Lord came down to live in the praises of Israel (see Psalm 22:3).

3. Before you ask for something, make sure you worship the Lord first. Then He will come to you with His presence.

E. THE ANGELS GAZED ON GOD

1. "And the cherubim shall stretch out their wings above, covering the mercy seat with their wings, and they shall face one another; the faces of the cherubim shall be toward the mercy seat" (Exodus 25:20, NKJV). Those closest to God want to __________ upon Him.

2. Their gaze was toward each other, but each __________ looking at the other. Their gaze was __________ God.

3. On the top, or lid of the Ark, the __________________ is the place on earth where God sat. "And there I will meet with thee, and I will commune with thee" (Exodus 25:22, KJV).

4. Prayer is how we look at God. We must be close to Him if we are to see Him __________ and know Him __________.

F. ANGELS REACHING OUT TO GOD

1. "The cherubims shall stretch forth their wings on high, covering the mercy seat with their wings" (Exodus 25:20, KJV).

2. Your outward body reflects your __________________. You give praise to God with your hands.

3. As I came to the conclusion, I asked the question, "*What shall we do?*"

4. I said, dramatically, "*WE MUST FALL ON OUR FACE BEFORE GOD!*" And they did!

PART THREE

21 DAYS OF PRAYER AND FASTING

POWERPOINT GUIDE

Slide 1 of 39

Slide 2 of 39

A. CHRISTIAN FASTING IS A NON-REQUIRED DISCIPLINE

Jesus said, "When you fast" (Matthew 6:16). Did Jesus mean you must fast, or did He give you an option? "If you fast?" Christian fasting is described:

1. Alters your diet, or
2. Eliminates food and/or drink
3. For a biblical purpose,
4. Accompanied with prayer.

Slide 3 of 39

B. RICHARD FOSTER SAID THERE HAS NOT BEEN A SIGNIFICANT WORK ON FASTING IN 100 YEARS. WHY?

1. Boomers.
2. Addiction / food.
3. No revival.
4. Need discipline and character.
5. Abundance of food has isolated us from realities of hunger.
6. Not healthier.
7. No testimony.
8. Growth of demonic forces.

Slide 4 of 39

C. HOW TO BEGIN FASTING

1. Ask God to lead you in your fast. Jesus describes fasting in the context of the Lord's Prayer – Matt. 6:9-15. "When ye fast, be not . . . of a sad countenance . . . but anoint thy head, and wash thy face, that thou appear not unto men to fast" (Matt. 6:16-18, *KJV*).
   a. Private for a personal request.
   b. Joint for a group project.

Slide 5 of 39

2. Write out your purpose, plan and length.

Slide 6 of 39

3. Begin with a one day fast, i.e., the Yom Kippur, Day of Atonement Fast. "On the tenth day of the seventh month of each year, you must go without eating to show sorrow for your sins" (Lev. 16:29, *CEV*). The Yom Kippur Fast is from sundown to sundown (Jewish day).
   a. If the issue is greater than a one-day fast; try fasting one day a week for 3 weeks or 7 weeks.
   b. Better to take small steps and succeed, than a giant step and fail.

Slide 7 of 39

4. Eat a light snack before sundown (English high tea). 

5. Dedicate time for meals to prayer. 

6. Bring Bible, books, notes, etc., (see specific fast). 

Slide 8 of 39

D. VARIOUS KINDS OF FASTS

1. One day fast – Yom Kippur fast.

2. Three day fast – Esther fast.

3. Ten day fast – Daniel.

4. Twenty-one day fast – Daniel.

5. Fasting from sweets and deserts.

Slide 9 of 39

6. The Daniel fast – eating only vegetables, no meat, sweets, etc.

7. Fasting from coffee, stimulants, etc.

8. Give up sports, hobbies, i.e., golf, tennis, etc.

9. Give up television, newspapers, etc.

10. Add your fast ________________________________.

When things and events are given up,
spend this extra time in prayer, Bible reading, etc.

Slide 10 of 39

E. PRACTICAL HELP TO BEGIN

General Checklist

Purpose: ________________________________

Fast: What you will withhold ________________________________

Begin: Date ________________ Time ________________

End: Date ________________ Time ________________

Vow: I believe God is the only answer to my request and that prayer without fasting is not enough to get an answer to my need. Therefore, by faith I am fasting because I need God to work in this matter.

Bible Basis: My Bible promise ________________________________

Resources: What I need during this fast ________________________________

God being my strength and grace being my basis, I commit myself to the above fast.

________________   ________________
Signed   Date

Slide 11 of 39

Lesson 2
How To Fast

Slide 12 of 39

A. WHAT IS FASTING?

1. Christian fasting is a non-required discipline that:
   a. Alters your diet,
   b. Eliminates food and/or drink,
   c. For a biblical purpose,
   d. Accompanied with prayer.

Slide 13 of 39

B. KINDS OF FASTS

1. The Normal fast is going without food for a certain period of time, drinking only liquid (water and/or juice).

2. The Absolute fast, no water or food at all. Should be short.

3. The Partial fast, omitting certain foods on a schedule of limited eating, i.e., only one meal a day, only vegetables, etc.

Slide 14 of 39

4. The Wesley fast is eating only bread (whole grains) and water.

5. The Rotation fast is eating or omitting certain families of food for a designated time. Some food is eaten every day. The Mayo Clinic fast is eating only one food group a day, omitting the other food groups, used as medical research to determine reaction (allergies) to a particular food group.

6. The Supernatural fast.

Slide 15 of 39

C. THE NINE FASTS IN SCRIPTURES

"Is this not the fast that I have chosen: to loose the bonds of wickedness, to undo the heavy burdens, to let the oppressed go free, and that you break every yoke? Is it not to share your bread with the hungry, and that you bring to your house the poor who are cast out; when you see the naked, that you cover him, and not hide yourself from your own flesh? Then your light shall break forth like the morning, your healing shall spring forth speedily, and your righteousness shall go before you; the glory of the Lord shall be your rear guard" (Isaiah 58:6-8).

Slide 16 of 39

D. WHAT FASTS ACCOMPLISH

1. The Apostle's Fast:
   - ➢ Issue: To free oneself from addiction to sin.
   - ➢ Verse: "This kind goeth not out but by prayer and fasting" (Matthew 17:21, *KJV*).

2. The Ezra Fast:
   - ➢ Issue: To solve problems.
   - ➢ Verse: "So we fasted and entreated our God for this, and He answered our prayer" (Ezra 8:22).

Slide 17 of 39

3. The Samuel Fast:
   - ➢ Issue: To bring evangelism and revival.
   - ➢ Verse: "So they gathered together at Mizpah, drew water, and poured it out before the Lord. And they fasted that day" (1 Samuel 7:6).

4. The Elijah Fast:
   - ➢ Issue: To solve emotional and mental problems.
   - ➢ Verse: "He (Elijah) . . . went in the strength of that meat forty days" (1 Kings 19:8).

Slide 18 of 39

5. The Widow's Fast:
   - ➢ Issue: To provide for physical needs of others.
   - ➢ Verse: "Is it (the fast) not to share your bread with the hungry?" (Isaiah 58:7).

6. The Saint Paul Fast:
   - ➢ Issue: To make life-changing decisions.
   - ➢ Verse: "He was three days without sight, and neither ate nor drank" (Acts 9:9).

Slide 19 of 39

7. The Daniel Fast:
   - ➢ Issue: For physical health or healing.
   - ➢ Verse: "Test your servants ten days . . . give us vegetables to eat and water to drink" (Daniel 1:12).

8. The John the Baptist Fast:
   - ➢ Issue: For your testimony.
   - ➢ Verse: "He will be great in the sight of the Lord, and shall drink neither wine nor strong drink" (Luke 1:15).

Slide 20 of 39

9. The Esther Fast:
   - ➢ Issue: For protection from the evil one.
   - ➢ Verse: "Gather all the Jews . . . fast for me; neither eat nor drink for three days, night or day. My maiden and I will fast likewise" (Esther 4:16).

Slide 21 of 39

Lesson 3

Fasting To Know God Intimately

Slide 22 of 39

A. GOD TOUCHED 8,000 PENTECOSTAL PREACHERS

1. Ed Silvoso of Harvest Evangelism invited me to del Plata, Argentina to speak to approximately 8,000 pastors, the largest gathering of Pentecostal preachers I had ever addressed.

2. The preacher before me motivated the crowd, there were shouts of "HALLELUJAH!" and "PRAISE THE LORD!"

Slide 23 of 39

3. Five men approached me. "We have read your book on fasting . . . and have come to pray for God to use you. They laid hands on me and prayed quietly over me.

4. A well-dressed lady spoke cultured English, who was a Supreme Court Justice in Argentina that was a believer. She said, "God told me to interpret for you today. Would you permit it?"

5. A small elderly lady holding a basin and a bottle of water and a towel asked, "May I wash your feet to prepare you for ministry?"

Slide 24 of 39

6. "I must go to the platform immediately," I explained. "But I receive your blessing." God could see her heart and blessed my sermon.

7. Silvoso said, "God spoke to me this morning. You should not preach on fasting today, but you must speak on knowing God intimately."

8. Inwardly I prayed again, *Jesus, help me!*

9. I remembered something I had written just a couple of weeks earlier.

B. HOW TO GET INTIMATE WITH GOD

1. If you are going to become intimate with God, you must get close to God. And no one has ever been closer to God than the two-angels on the lid of the Ark of the Covenant.

2. "You shall make a mercy seat of pure gold; two and a half cubits shall be its length and a cubit and a half its width. And you shall make two cherubim of gold; of hammered work you shall make them at the two ends of the mercy seat" (Exodus 25:17-18).

3. The Ark was about the size of a chest, and its lid was called the mercy seat. God sat on a box, not a throne. The word "ark" means *box*.

4. Located on the right and left sides were two angels sculptured of pure gold. Pure gold suggests holiness.

5. Gold has several degrees of purity, 24-karat gold being the purest.

6. The angels were pure gold, because God wants purity in the lives of those who worship Him and are close to Him.

7. The difference between pure gold and a lesser grade of gold is fire – and the hotter the purifying fire, the more dross and impurities are burned away.

8. Sludge floats to the top, and is skimmed away, leaving refined gold.

9. God uses the fire of suffering and difficulties to rid us of impurities.

10. Sometimes God allows physical failures, financial reverse, or family difficulties.

11. Fire burns away the impurity of greed and self, and other sins.

12. First, God touches our fleshly sins and other outward problems.

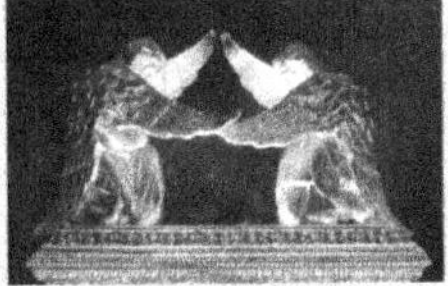

13. Next, God focuses on any inward sins that hinder your walk with Him.

14. Why did God demand that the angels and the mercy seat be made of pure God? Because He Himself was going to sit there. God is pure, so He would not sit there if the mercy seat and the angels were made of impure gold.

15. How pure is pure gold? The goldsmith will know when he looks into a mirror of gold to see his own face.

C. ANGELS WERE SCULPTED

1. Two worshiping angels were sculpted from a piece of gold – not poured into a mold but beaten into the proper form. "And thou shalt make two cherubims of gold, of beaten work shalt thou make them, in the two ends of the mercy seat" (Exodus 25:18, *KJV*).

2. The purer the gold, the easier it would be for the craftsman to sculpt them.

3. They are literally shaped by hand into the worshiping position.

4. When you are pure, you have separated yourself from sin, i.e., you are holy. When you are sculpted – or beaten with hammers – you become yielded to God.

5. Things that are poured into the same mold become identical, something sculpted is unique.

6. Each of us is a little different from the other. All of us are fashioned by the hands of the same Master Craftsman.

7. The sculptor puts his *personality and talent* into what he forms.

8. The Master Craftsman puts unique life – *His life* – and design into you when He shapes you into a worshiper.

9. What kind of *hammer* does God use on you? A different hammer on greed, and an entirely different hammer on lust.

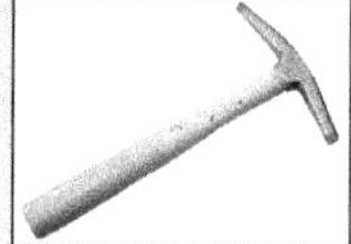

Slide 33 of 39

10. If you won't allow the *Lord* to use His hammer on you, then something else or someone else will have to beat you into submission.

11. God doesn't want to break you, but to *bend* your heart to His will. "But we all, with unveiled face, beholding as in a mirror the glory of the Lord, are being transformed into the same image from glory to glory, just as by the Spirit of the Lord" (2 Corinthians 3:18, *NKJV*).

Slide 34 of 39

D. SPREAD WINGS TO WORSHIP

1. The angels outstretched wings reminds us of worshipers stretching out their hands in *praise to God*.

2. God *dwelt* between the outstretched wings of the angels. The Lord came down to live in the praises of Israel (see Psalm 22:3).

3. Before you ask for something make sure you worship the Lord first. Then He will come to you with His presence.

Slide 35 of 39

E. THE ANGELS GAZED ON GOD

1. "And the cherubim shall stretch out their wings above, covering the mercy seat with their wings, and they shall face one another; the faces of the cherubim shall be toward the mercy seat" (Exodus 25:20, *NKJV*). Those closest to God want to *gaze* upon Him.

2. Their gaze was toward each other, but each *was not* looking at the other. Their gaze was *upon* God.

Slide 36 of 39

3. On the top, or lid of the Ark, the *mercy seat* is the place on earth where God sat. "And there I will meet with thee, and I will commune with thee" (Exodus 25:22, *KJV*).

4. Prayer is how we look at God. We must be close to Him if we are to see Him *clearly* and know Him *intimately*.

Slide 37 of 39

F. ANGELS REACHING OUT TO GOD

1. The cherubims shall stretch forth their wings on high, covering the mercy seat with their wings" (Exodus 25:20, *KJV*).

2. Your outward body reflects your *inner soul*. You give praise to God with your hands.

Slide 38 of 39

3. As I came to the conclusion, I asked the question, *"What shall we do?"*

4. I said, dramatically, *"WE MUST FALL ON OUR FACE BEFORE GOD!"* And they did!

Slide 39 of 39

PART FOUR

21 DAYS OF
PRAYER AND FASTING

21 DAILY DEVOTIONS

WHAT FASTING IS AND HOW TO GET STARTED

YOU may know something about fasting, but never tried it. Or, perhaps you have fasted, but it was not an effective experience. In this first week, let us go back to the basics. Let's ask some basic questions. What is fasting? What happens when I fast? Why am I fasting? These basic answers will point you in the right direction. Like every new discipline, whether sports or learning a new procedure at work, take it slowly and master each step as you move along. Remember, your fasting is associated with praying. Since prayer is establishing a relationship with God, your emphasis is not the food you withhold from your body. It is your prayers that come from your heart.

Day 1	Finding God's Presence
Day 2	Fasting Is Demonstrating Faith
Day 3	Fasting Is Obedience
Day 4	Fasting and Prayer
Day 5	Fasting Is About God
Day 6	Fasting Is a Yielded Heart
Day 7	Fasting for a Purpose

Day 1

FINDING GOD'S PRESENCE

"This is the kind of fasting I want...then when you call,
I will answer, 'Yes, I am here.' he will quickly reply."

Isaiah 58:6, 9, NLT

FASTING is setting aside food, entertainment, and all those things you think you must do. Fasting is the discipline where you seek the presence of God to find His perfect peace. Fasting calls you to set aside time for the Lord and to set aside pleasure and things that satisfy the outward life. Get quiet before the Lord to listen for His voice. He will speak to you in your conscience. He will also speak in His Word. Read His Word, lots of Scripture...then pray as you pour over Scriptures, "Lord speak to me, I need to hear from You." Only as you tune out distractions...noise... and the radio and television...and food, are you ready to hear God speak.

Lord, I will fast in Your presence and wait to hear Your Holy Spirit speak to me. I will read much Scripture and meditate on Your Word. Then I will pray. I will ask You for the request upon my heart because You are nearby to listen. I am here. Amen.

Fasting is only a discipline to help you reach out to God. Don't trust in your fasting for answers. Fasting is only as effective as your praying heart. Don't think that you will get an answer because you fasted a long time—even 40 days—saying "No" to all pleasure and entertainment. Fasting is only as effective as your open relationship with the Lord. If there is anything blocking your approach to God, get rid of it, fast and seek the Lord now!

Lord, forgive me when I fast to brag to others or fast to please myself. Cleanse me of the sin of pride. Fill me with the Holy Spirit for effective fasting and fellowship and talking to You. Amen.

READING:

Isaiah 58:1-14

Key Thought: Fasting as a discipline will not get prayers answered; fasting is only a discipline to reach out to God. It is your relationship with God that will get answers to your prayer request.

REFLECTION

FASTING IS DEMONSTRATING FAITH

*"On the tenth day of the seventh month of each years you must go
without eating to show sorrow for your sins."*

Leviticus 16:29, CEV

SINCE you are going to fast, learn some basic truths from the first time fasting is mentioned in Scriptures. It is called "The Day of Atonement Fast," the annual day when the high priest "sacrificed the goat for the sins of the people" (Lev. 16:15, CEV). Just because blood was shed, it did not cover all the people of Israel. Each individual had to demonstrate faith in their heart and also show the sorrow of repentance by fasting the whole Day of Atonement. When God saw their act of personal faith and the blood shed for forgiveness, God accepted them and cleansed their sins. Your faith is more than speaking words to God, it is the response of the heart in a decision that influences your eternal life.

*Lord, I humbly come to You on this day of fasting. My heart desire is more than the words
I speak. I am praying and fasting for an answer to my request. Hear my prayers and show
me Your will. Amen.*

Jesus confirmed the necessity of both when He said, "This kind does not go out except by prayer and fasting" (Matt. 17:21, NKJV). So fasting by itself does not work, it takes both fasting (not eating) and faith-inspired prayers. So pray every time you feel hunger pangs, and at the same time when you are supposed to eat or you feel the desire to eat—pray.

Lord, my request is important. Therefore, I am putting my request first. I will pray for an answer and I will wait to eat until my time of fasting is up. Then I will give thanks for food. Amen.

READING:

Leviticus 16:1-29;

Matthew 17:14-21

Key Thought: The first time God commanded fasting was to demonstrate faith in God for forgiveness of sins and answer to their prayers.

REFLECTION

Day 3

FASTING IS OBEDIENCE

*"When you fast, don't make it obvious as the hypocrites...
so people will admire them for fasting."*

Matthew 6:16, NLT

IN one of the first recorded sermons Jesus commanded, "When you fast." It seems clear that Jesus expected His followers to fast. Have you fasted one day in obedience to Jesus' command? He didn't say, "If" you fast, as though you had the choice. He didn't tell you how often too fast, nor did He tell you what food to withhold, nor did He tell what to pray when fasting. His command was very clear, "When you fast." The basic ingredient of fasting is *relationship*. This is when you and God spend time together. You can fast when facing an emergency or fast when praying for a request. But don't forget you fast to worship God...to praise God...to thank Him for all He has done for you. What would be your main reasons for fasting?

> *Lord, I come just to tell You I love You. I have told You before, but I need to tell You again and again because Your love continues each and every day. I need to tell You I love You because my selfish, sinful nature constantly tends to get me to think only of myself. Amen.*

Jesus reminds us there would be hypocrites who fast for the wrong reasons. Some do it for attention from others and some do it for inner selfish reasons. Since there can be wrong attitudes to fast, make sure you fast with the right attitude. And what is that? "That you may know Christ and make Him known" (see Phil. 3:10-14).

Lord, I am fasting to know You and please You. When my attitude gets mixed up, forgive me. When my mind wanders, bring me back. I want You to be number one in my life...help me keep this promise. Amen.

READING:

Matthew 6:16-34;

Philippians 3:10-14

Key Thought: There are wrong attitudes when fasting that will negate the reason why you fast.

REFLECTION

Day 4

FASTING AND PRAYER

"Hannah began crying and refused to eat...please let me have a son."

1 Samuel 1:7, 11, CEV

WHAT comes first, fasting or prayer? Hannah wanted a son so badly that she couldn't eat, so she prayed. The urge in her heart came first. As you get ready to fast, is there an urge in your heart that you want God to hear and answer. If that need is there, then fast about it. This has been called the Samuel Fast. There are some people who want to lose weight so badly they diet. In the spiritual realm, you have a burden—it is something you want God to do. The burden comes first, then fast and pray for God to answer. God is not impressed just because you stop eating—God is impressed with a broken heart (Joel 2:13).

Lord, teach me how to fast and pray. Keep me from emphasizing "not eating." Help me see You in my fast and keep my focus on faith and praying. Give me a pure heart. Amen.

Hannah's need was real—she wanted a son. But she was barren—childless. So, her need drove her to God. She lost her appetite, then asked God to give her a son. Does God hear the sincere prayer when accompanied with fasting? "The Lord blessed Elkanah and Hannah with a son. She named him Samuel" (Is. 1:19-20, CEV). The name *Samuel* means "to ask."

Lord, I do not trust "fasting," that is just legalism. I trust You. My prayer is my relationship with You is the reason I fast. You are the basis of answered prayer. I trust You. Amen.

READING:

1 Samuel 4:1-28

Key Thought: Hannah is an example of one who was burdened for an answer from God and she expressed it in fasting.

REFLECTION

Day 5

FASTING IS ABOUT GOD

"'Turn to Me now...come with fasting, weeping and mourning....'
Return to the Lord your God... I will pour out My Spirit upon all flesh."

Joel 2:12-13, 28, NLT

DO you need personal reviving? Has your Christian group with whom you live and minister lost its enthusiasm and spiritual energy? What can turn around an individual or a group? Prayer and fasting. When you go without eating before God, you demonstrate your dedication to Him. You are saying God is more important than enjoying yourself with food. God is even more important than the necessary strength you get from food. You are saying He is important—God is more necessary than food, and He is more satisfying than the most enjoyable food. When you fast, you are sacrificing to God your enjoyment and necessary strength. Would you do that for God?

Lord, You are the most important person in my life; I will give up food for You. Lord, You are the most enjoyable person in my life; I will give up pleasure for You. Why? Because I get my strength in life from You and I get my satisfaction in life from You. Amen.

Fasting is not about food. It is about God. Paul declared, "For to me, to live is Christ" (Phil. 1:21, NKJV). That is much better than those who say, "For me to live is food" or "for me to live is pleasure." When you make the Lord number one in your life, you are entering the "victorious Christian life."

Lord, I look to You for my spiritual strength, so I will seek You with all my heart. I look to You for physical strength, so after my fast I will return to healthy food and healthy exercise. Amen.

READING:

Joel 2:12-37

Key Thought: The key to spiritual revival in individuals and groups is putting God first in everything, including food and pleasure.

REFLECTION

Day 6

FASTING IS A YIELDED HEART

"What good is fasting when you keep on fighting and quarreling?...
You humble yourselves by going through the motions of penance....
Is this what you call fasting?"

Isaiah 58:4-5, NLT

GOD doesn't look at your stomach when you fast, He looks at your heart. He will not answer because you are hungry for food. You must hunger for His presence and thirst for His answer to your request. Isaiah 58 has the full reference to fasting in Scripture. It tells you what not to do, and it reveals wrong motives for fasting. In verses 6 and 7, God gives correct heart attitudes for fasting. Then He says, "Then when you call, the Lord will answer. 'Yes, I am here'" (58:9). Since God says He will answer and His presence will come to you...are you ready to fast and pray?

Lord, I come asking for forgiveness for my pride and selfish ways. I have fasted and prayed. Forgive me! I need Your help! I need Your presence! I need it now! Amen.

There are not a lot of printed prayers for fasting. There is not a list of things to do and prohibitions to avoid. God wants you to have a humble heart before Him. He wants a yielded spirit to learn and become what He teaches in Scriptures. He wants an obedient servant to be faithful to Him and obedient to the Word of God.

Lord, I am listening for Your inner voice to guide me. I will learn Your Scripture verses to teach me what to do. I yield to the Holy Spirit to fill me with wisdom and power for service. I am ready. Amen.

READING:

Isaiah 58:1-14

Key Thought: Fasting is not about the food or drink you withhold, it is about your yielded spirit to God, your inquiring mind to learn, and your obedient service to Him.

REFLECTION

Day 7

FASTING FOR A PURPOSE

"There by the Ahava Canal, I gave orders for all of us to fast and humble ourselves before our God. We prayed that he would give us a safe journey and protect us."

Ezra 8:21, NLT

THE people of Israel faced a dangerous trip of approximately 1,000 miles through hostile territories to return to their homeland. They fasted and prayed for three days for a safe trip. When something scares you—really terrifies you—then fast for God's protection. But refraining from food alone wasn't the answer. Ezra was praying for "God's hand of protection" (v. 22). Notice who fasted: "all of us." God is moved when His people demonstrate unity. "Where two or three are gathered together in My name" (Matt. 18:20, NKJV). Also notice where they gathered: "before our God." Your church is a good place to gather and pray, and so is your home. Actually, you can fast and pray any place. The answer, "There am I in the midst" (Matt. 18:20, KJV).

Lord, I am afraid of what might happen. I pray to You and demonstrate my faith by fasting and praying for an answer. I come in privacy before You, but I will also seek out others who are concerned to fast and pray with me. Amen.

Ezra demonstrated spiritual leadership by calling for a fast—God's anointed symbol of trusting Him for an answer to their coming danger. Notice they fasted and prayed before they faced danger, not during danger, or even after the danger was over. Isn't this putting God first in everything even in seeking protection. What happened? Ezra testified, "He heard our prayers" (see Ezra 8:23).

Lord, teach me priority, i.e., that You come first in everything including prayer for protection. I pray for protection in my life from danger that I am ignorant of, and that which has not threatened me yet. Thank You for the future answer. Amen.

READING:

Ezra 8:15-36

Key Thought: Ezra called a fast of all those he was leading before they faced coming danger.

REFLECTION

Week Two

WHAT FASTING IS ALL ABOUT

YOU have been fasting for the past week. You probably had some days that were easier than others. Remember, fasting is putting aside how much you eat, or when you eat, or maybe your fast is elimination of something else in your life. Remember, it is the prayers that come out of your heart that matters.

Day 8   Fasting When You Need God

Day 9   Doorway to God

Day 10   Saying "Yes"

Day 11   Waiting and Listening

Day 12   Life Changing

Day 13   Everything New Begins with Fasting

Day 14   Your Duty to Fast

Finish this week of fasting with enthusiasm and faith. "But without faith *it is* impossible to please *Him,* for he who comes to God must believe that He is, and *that* He is a rewarder of those who diligently seek Him" (Heb. 11:6, NKJV). Faith is more than knowing that God exists, it is acting on what you know about God and obeying what God has said. Your obedience begins with fasting and looking to Him. Now, end your fast with your eyes still fixed on Him.

Day 8

FASTING WHEN YOU NEED GOD

"Turn to Me now, while there is time...come with fasting, weeping, and mourning. ...Then, after doing all those things I will pour out My Spirit."

Joel 2:12, 28, NLT

THERE were special days in the life of Israel when God told them to fast, such as the Day of Atonement. But when followers had an urgent need, they could also fast. Then when they felt spiritually empty, they could fast to find their way into God's presence. It was then God would pour His Spirit on His people. Sometimes a fast can lead to a great revival such as the First Great Awakening in the 1700s or the worldwide revival of 1906-07. Then again, individuals have fasted for personal revival. They have been filled with the Spirit or re-energized for a special ministry. What could happen to you if you fasted and God poured His Spirit on you?

Lord, I come into Your presence fasting. I am not seeking a great answer, and I do not have a great need; I come seeking You. I want to know You better...deeper than ever before. My fast is centered on You. Amen.

Today's verse describes weeping and mourning. That is not an emotional response to an emergency or some outward reason for fasting. Look within your heart. Ask God to show you how selfish your actions are or how egotistical your thoughts. When you see yourself as God sees you...you will weep and mourn. Especially when you see God's glory and holiness.

Lord, when I see my heart (Jer. 17:9) as You see it, I thank You for Your forgiveness of my sin and I praise You for Your mercy. When I see my sin, I bow to worship You in holiness. Amen.

READING:

Jeremiah 17:1-10;

Joel 2:12-32

Key Thought: God has provided the discipline of fasting for you to gain entrance into His presence.

REFLECTION

Day 9

DOORWAY TO GOD

*"I, Daniel, had been in mourning for three whole weeks.
All that time I had eaten no rich food. No meat or wine
crossed my lips...until those three weeks had passed."*

Daniel 10:2-3, NLT

FASTING is a *doorway* into the presence of God. Daniel had been fasting and praying for 21 days when the angel came to assure him God had heard his prayer. The enemy was fighting against Daniel. The enemy was a demon, the prince of Persia. Apparently, every nation has a chief demon that carries out the devil's agenda. Daniel had been faithful to continue in prayer, so God sent an angel to tell Him what would happen in that country and to His people. When you start fasting, satan is your enemy in your spiritual battle. But God has angels who will fight for you. Who will win? It depends on your commitment to fast, pray, believe in faith, and to ask continually. Are you ready to fast and pray to enter the doorway into God's presence?

Lord, I am weak spiritually and my faith is not strong. Increase my faith (Luke 17:5). I will fast and seek Your presence for my answers. I will enter spiritual warfare (Eph. 6:10-18) and will continue praying till I get my answer (Luke 18:1). And with Your help, I will not faint. Amen.

No one said fasting was easy. It may be one of the hardest of all spiritual disciplines. But, if you want victory over the evil one, you must first conquer your fleshly desires and control your appetite and desires. It is not wrong to eat; God gave you enjoyable food to get strength to work each day. But, fasting puts God first. When you seek first His kingdom, and righteousness, you win a spiritual victory (Matt. 6:33). Then enjoy food after you finish your fast and win your battle.

Lord, because my need is great, I will fast for 21 days. I vow to continue praying until You answer my request. I am not strong spiritually, nor do I have great faith. Give me courage and strength to reach the end of my fast. Amen.

READING:

Daniel 10:1-21;

Luke 18:1-8

Key Thought: Daniel fasted for 21 days before he got an answer from God. Fasting has a time limit that challenges us to pray until the time is accomplished.

REFLECTION

Day 10

SAYING "YES"

*"Turn to me now…give me your hearts. Come with
fasting, weeping, and mourning. Don't tear your clothing
in your grief, but tear your hearts instead."*

Joel 2:12-13, NLT

P EOPLE immediately identify fasting with the "No" word…no food…no television…no snacks. The "No" word cuts you off from people and draws you into a tiny circle of people who live like you. Don't get me wrong, you need to say "No" sometimes to people, and to food and to snacks. Think of fasting as the "Yes" word. You are saying "Yes" to God, "Yes" to answered prayer, and "Yes" to a bigger ministry. The greatest thing about fasting is you are drawing a line in the sand and saying, "No!" It's "No" on one side, but fasting on the other side says, "Yes." You say "Yes" to fellowship with God and isn't Christianity about *relationship*? Yes, fasting is good because it is where you find the presence of God.

Lord, I don't want to be a negative person. I want to say "Yes" to You. I want Your blessings in my life…Your protection…Your fellowship…. Yes, I want to do what You want me to do. Amen.

Fasting has many lessons to teach you. When you say "No" to the temptation of food for a short while, you say "Yes" to God's presence. You say "Yes" to answered prayers and "Yes" to many unknown opportunities. As a matter of fact, you say "Yes" to worship. You worship God in a way greater than ever. Right now would be a great time to stop and worship.

Lord, I begin by thanking You for a free will that can say "Yes" and "No." Thank You for showing me dangers and things that can harm. I say "No" to them. I say "Yes" to Your greatness in my life. Lead me to greater worship." Amen.

READING:

Psalm 147;

Daniel 1:1-21

Key Thought: There is a "No" to fasting but don't focus on the negative; look at the benefits and blessings when you say "Yes" to fasting.

REFLECTION

Day 11

WAITING AND LISTENING

*"Call to Me, and I will answer you, and show you great and
mighty things, which you do not know."*

Jeremiah 33:3, NKJV

"Wait for the Promise of the Father."

Acts 1:4, NKJV

FASTING is your path to answered prayers. As you present your requests to your loving heavenly Father, you may have to wait for an answer. Sometimes God says, "No" (Acts 16:6), other times He says, "Yes" (Acts 16:9). But there are times He says, "Wait." Jesus has promised to give you everything you ask in His name (John 14:13-14). Sometimes you find your requests are not being answered. Fasting gives you time to wait in the Father's presence for answers (Ps. 37:7). Fasting takes your focus off your bodily needs and places all attention on God. Fasting quiets your whole system down so you can hear from God. Are you waiting and listening?

Lord, I bow in Your presence to worship and wait. I tune my ears to listen and learn. I quietly look for answers from You. Amen.

The discipline of fasting will help you get answers from God. Is there sin that will block your communication with God (Ps. 66:18)? Have you searched the Word to make sure the requests are biblical (John 15:7)? Are your requests mixed with faith (Mark 11:20-24)? Is your request time-related?

Sometimes God says wait. Are the answers you seek within the will of God? If not, God's answer may be "No"! Remember, God has a plan for your life; it is not to hurt you, but to give you His happiness (Jer. 29:11).

Lord, because my need is great, I will fast. I vow to continue praying until You answer my request. I am not strong spiritually, nor do I have great faith; give me courage and strength to reach the end of my fast. Amen.

READING:

Jeremiah 29:1-9;

Acts 1:1-13

Key Thought: Fasting alone will not guarantee any answers to your prayer, but fasting may help you find why the request is not immediately fulfilled.

REFLECTION

Day 12

LIFE CHANGING

"Moses remained there on the mountain with the Lord forty days and forty nights. In all that time he ate no bread and drank no water. ...When Moses came down...he wasn't aware that his face had become radiant."

Exodus 34:28-29, NLT

FASTING can change your life, just as Moses' life was changed after fasting 40 days. It was not fasting that changed Moses, it was God's presence. Moses "had spoken to the Lord" (Ex. 34:30, *ELT*). When you have been in the presence of the Lord—talking to Him face to face—you will be changed. It wasn't fasting that changed Moses, it was God's glory reflected in him. Now, your face won't light up like a light bulb, but your testimony will reveal God. People will know it. And the longer you stay in God's presence, the greater your life will be changed. Has fasting changed your life? If not, let God change your life.

Lord, I no longer seek food and earthly pleasure. I seek Your presence. Change me into Your likeness. Make me shine for Jesus' sake. It is not about fasting, it is about You! Amen.

Fasting is a limited human discipline that will help you find God's presence. You cannot fast 40 days without water like Moses; you will permanently harm yourself if you don't drink within 7 days. Your body is over 70% water. Don't try going more than 3 days without water. Moses' fast was a supernatural miracle. You cannot do what he did, and your facial skin will not shine as his, but you can experience God's presence as Moses did. How much would you like for your testimony to shine?

Lord, I don't fast to shine, I fast to find Your presence. I don't fast to get answers to prayer, I fast to worship You and glorify You. Be glorified in my fast—in my prayer—and in my sacrifice. Amen.

READING:

Exodus 35:27-35;

2 Corinthians 3:1-18

Key Thought: Fasting does not change your life; it puts you in the presence of God, and He will change your life.

REFLECTION

Day 13

EVERYTHING NEW BEGINS WITH FASTING

*"Then Samuel told them, 'Gather all of Israel to Mizpah, and I will pray to the
Lord for you.' So they gathered at Mizpah and, in a great ceremony, drew water
from a well and poured it out before the Lord. They also went without food
all day and confessed that they had sinned against the Lord."*

1 Samuel 7:5-6, NLT

THE book of Judges tells how Israel kept rejecting God and He judged them for their sins, but in His mercy, He sent a "Judge" to lead them to repentance and restoration. Samuel was the last judge; he introduced the kings and their rule over God's people. Samuel began by calling the nation to repentance with fasting. This experience changed everything. Note the phrase "great ceremony" as evident by three significant symbols. First, Samuel poured out water symbolizing pouring out their heart in repentance. Second, they fasted, symbolic of self-denial and hungering for God's presence. Third, Samuel offered a "whole burnt offering" (v. 9), symbolic of cleansing from sin by a blood offering.

Lord, I come confessing my sin against You. I will repent publicly—where required—and vow inwardly to live for You. I fast to show my denial of self, living and hungering for Your presence. Hear me and be with me! Amen.

No celebration is great if we don't recognize the blood of Jesus Christ cleanses us from all sin (1 John 1:9). Samuel offered a lamb and the people identified with its forgiveness of sin by fasting. Just as God prepared His people spiritually to become a great nation, so God wants to prepare you for spiritual greatness in personal growth and outward ministry.

Lord, I will do everything necessary to grow in Christ and be a more effective servant. I fast to yield my old way and seek Your presence to gain Your blessing and power in ministry. Amen.

READING:

1 Samuel 7:1-17;

Isaiah 58:6-11

Key Thought: When you are backslidden and spiritually bankrupt, fast, repent, and seek God's presence for spiritual blessings.

REFLECTION

Day 14

YOUR DUTY TO FAST

*"[Israel] gathered at Mizpah...went without food (fasted) all day and
confessed that they had sinned against the Lord. ...When the Philistine rulers
heard that Israel had gathered...they mobilized their army and advanced. ...
Samuel pleaded with the Lord to help Israel, and the Lord answered him."*

1 Samuel 7:6-9, NLT

THE people fasted, repented, and called on the Lord. Then the enemy attacked. That may happen to you when you fast. Notice what the leader Samuel did: he "pleaded with the Lord" (v. 9). Are you a leader? Then you must fast with the people. You must be covered by the blood of the sacrificial Lamb (Jesus), and you must fast even as Samuel fasted. Remember fasting puts many spiritual forces into motion—both by God and satan—so you must pray for yourself and for others. What did Samuel do? He "cried unto the Lord for Israel" (v. 9).

Lord, fasting is more than self-discipline to make me strong. Fasting uncovers the devil's attacks against me. I pray first for protection for me, my family and my church. Then I pray for strength to stand strong for You. Finally, I pray for spiritual victory over evil and satan. Amen.

The Lord answered (Samuel's) prayer and made thunder crash around (the enemy). "The Philistines panicked and ran away" (v. 10, CEV). God will give you victory. "They were subdued...all the days of Samuel" (v. 13, NKJV). But this was not a final victory, they came back against King Saul and David. Just as Israel never got a final victory over the Philistines, so you will not get a final victory over sin and satan on earth. So fast and pray today and tomorrow and all the days until you see Jesus.

Lord, my victory today is not a final victory but the beginning of all victories over sin on earth. This victory is one of many to follow—so I fast today and will fast tomorrow and will fast till Jesus comes. Amen.

READING:

1 Samuel 7:3-13;

Revelation 19:11-21

Key Thought: Samuel and Israel fasted to get a victory over the Philistines; it was not the final victory, but the beginning of a lifelong struggle against sin until Jesus returns.

REFLECTION

FASTING TO KNOW AND WORSHIP GOD

THE success of fasting is not measured in what food you don't eat or how long you go without eating. Success is talking to God in prayer. It is when you know God and worship Him. The good thing about fasting, it gets your mind off what you will eat, how to make money, or your next project. The joy of fasting is enjoying your relationship with the Lord. The measure of fasting is talking and listening to God. If you get answers to your prayers, that is an additional bonus for enjoying His presence. Your answers are like your favorite dessert after a full meal.

Day 15   Fasting When Facing a Special Ministry

Day 16   Seeking God

Day 17   Worshiping God

Day 18   Hovering

Day 19   Receiving the Spirit

Day 20   Getting Ready

Day 21   When Fasting Is Good

Day 15

FAST WHEN FACING
A SPECIAL MINISTRY

"When this vision came to me, I, Daniel, had been in
mourning for three whole weeks. All that time I had eaten
no rich food. No meat or wine crossed my lips, and I used no
fragrant lotions until those three weeks had passed."

Daniel 10:2-3, NLT

DANIEL fasted and prayed for 21 days. It was not a complete fast from food. It was probably what is called today a Daniel Fast, which included vegetables only, without meat, rich foods, or special drinks—water only. Daniel was not fasting for health on this occasion, as he did in chapter 1. He was fasting about a vision (v. 1) God was giving him. In the same way, you may be fasting about your ministry or a special task God has for you. The Daniel Fast was not primarily for physical health—that was a byproduct. In the same way when you fast for ministry, you will get a healthier body to glorify God.

Lord, I will fast when facing a ministry challenge. I will spend more than one day fasting by
eliminating part of my diet. I do it for You and to make my prayers more focused. See what
I am doing and give me health and answer my request. Amen.

Sometimes you will fast when you or a group of intercessors are praying for the health of a sick person (James 5:13-15). You might give up all solid food for a one- or three-day fast. However, if you are fasting longer, you might follow the Daniel fast of vegetables only. Remember, it is not the withholding of food that God honors, it is your faith in Him and the depth of your praying that He answers.

Lord, thank You for supplying food that I must eat to live. Thank You for the desire and discipline to give up food for a period of time to pray and ask for answers from You. Thank You for the opportunity to fast from food to demonstrate faith to you. Amen.

READING:

Mark 9:14-29;

Daniel 10:1-14

Key Thought: When facing a special ministry, Daniel gave up all pleasant food to fast and prayed for God's answer.

REFLECTION

Day 16

SEEKING GOD

"But the time is coming—indeed it's here now—when true worshipers will worship the Father in spirit and in truth. The Father is looking for those who will worship him that way. For God is Spirit, so those who worship him must worship in spirit and in truth."

John 4:23-24, NLT

FASTING is a discipline that opens up worship. Have you had trouble getting in the mood to worship? Have you worshiped God and come away empty? Worship is not about methods, it's not about fasting, and it's not about praying. Worshiping is about God Himself. The old Scottish word for *worship* is *worthship*. How much is God worth to you? Are you more concerned about your feelings, or about answers, or about the way you pray, or the time and place you pray? Then you are missing the whole idea of worship. How much is God worth to you? Is God your life...liberty...and pursuit of happiness? Worship brings you back to the issue, "Why are you here?" and "What is the secret of life?" When you properly worship God, the answer to the first question is in the Westminster Catechism, "Why did God make you?" The purpose of all people is to worship God, glorify Him, and enjoy Him forever. Have you fulfilled God's purpose for your life?

Lord, I put You first in my prayers. I worship You. I put You first in my time; I begin the day worshiping You. I put You first in my marriage and resources. I give control of everything to You in worship. Amen.

What is fasting worth to you? If you fast for any other reason than to worship God, you are not living on the main track of God. Are you ssidetracked? If your prime concern in life is your financial worth, you have missed God's assessment. Your prime concern in life is to give God His true worth in praise and worship. Who is the most important person in your life?

Lord, I give You more than worship, I give you myself. I want to do more for You. I want to be a better Christian and give You even more worship. How can I give you more? Amen.

READING:

John 4:1-34

Key Thought: Worship focuses on God and giving Him the true worth for all He is and has done.

REFLECTION

Day 17

WORSHIPING GOD

*"David appointed the following...to lead...in worship before...
the Lord. ...Give thanks to the Lord and proclaim his greatness.
Let the whole world know what he has done."*

1 Chronicles 16:4,8 NLT

THE energy of fasting is found in worship. Fasting is more than not eating. Lots of people do that when they get sick, or they worry, or they diet. The energy of worship is focusing on God by making Him first in your life and praising Him for what He does for you. Worship God right now for saving you from hell and for giving you the light of the Holy Spirit so you can learn and find the secret of the mystery of life. Thank God for your parents, your culture, and your growth until now. Thank God for your health and how you are not as bad off as some. Thank God for your good mind to think, good emotions to find happiness, and for your will's ability to make proper decisions to direct your life. But most of all, thank God for the ability to know yourself. Think of the people who cannot make good decisions in life; they don't know who they are.

Lord, I thank You for forgiveness of my sins and answers to prayer and for the indwelling of Jesus Christ in my heart. Thank You for leading me in the past up to this moment. Thank You for giving me the ability to work and take care of myself and my family. Amen.

Worship is the whole reason why you fast. Fasting is nothing more than the ability to stop eating for enjoyment or strength. Make God your life—worship— and you will find happiness, you will find purpose in life, and you will discover the reason why you were born. Worship is not just a nice thing to do; worship is absolutely necessary to fulfill the reason why you were born. Worship is more than learning; worship is focusing on God Himself and God alone.

Lord, I worship You. You are the center of my life. I worship who You are, what You have done for me. How can I serve You? How can I worship better and more effectively? Amen.

READING:

1 Chronicles 16:1-43

Key Thought: Fasting is not about denying yourself food; fasting is focusing all your energy on worshiping God.

REFLECTION

Day 18

HOVERING

"And the Spirit of God was hovering over the surface of the water."

Genesis 1:2, NLT

"The glory of the Lord filled the tabernacle. ...The cloud (Shekinah)...
hovered over the tabernacle."

Exodus 40:34, 38, NLT

FASTING is not pretty, enjoyable, or fun. You never try fasting for itself. But the discipline of fasting makes you spiritually healthy. But when you fast properly for the right motive, then you open up God's world to you. Fasting can get God to *hover* over your life. "In the beginning God created the heavens and the earth" (Gen. 1:1, NKJV) when it was just a big red clay ball. "Then the Holy Spirit hovered over it" (Gen. 1:2, ELT). That word *hovered* is a picture of a mother bird sitting on her nest to turn eggs into living birds. Just as the Holy Spirit "hovers" to put life into everything on earth, so today, the Holy Spirit wants to "hover" over you to give you eternal life—abundant life—indwelling life (Gal. 2:20, John 14:20). You need to fast to get the Holy Spirit to "hover" over your life.

Lord, I will fast to seek Your presence for my life. I will fast to get rid of sin and any distractions in my life. I fast to seek You and You only. Holy Spirit, come hover over my life. Infuse spiritual life into me. Amen.

Fasting is a discipline that is not done for pleasure. Note David fasted and wept (2 Sam. 12:22). Israel fasted and mourned (Zech. 7:5). They afflicted themselves (Isa. 58:3). They tore their garments (Joel 2:13). Hannah was sorrowful (1 Sam. 1:15). Why put yourself through those difficulties? Fasting gets the Holy Spirit—God's presence—to hover over your life.

Lord, I seek Your peace and happiness. I am not naturally miserable, but I will fast to get Your presence. I will fast and discipline my desires so I will receive Your presence. Come hover over my life. Amen.

READING:

1 Samuel 1:1-2:5

Key Thought: As a result of fasting, God's Spirit will hover over your life.

REFLECTION

Day 19

RECEIVING THE SPIRIT

"Come with fasting, weeping and mourning. ...Then after
doing all those things, I will pour out My spirit upon all people."

Joel 2:12, 28, NLT

FASTING is a great invitation to you from the Lord. He promises that when you do all things associated with fasting, He will pour the Holy Spirit out on you. What would be better in your life than the Holy Spirit? Wouldn't that be better that a raise...promotion...vacation...a big new house? How much of the Holy Spirit do you want? The answer, "How much and how deep are you prepared to fast?" When do you want the Holy Spirit? The answer, "When and how long are you willing to fast?" What do you want to do for God? The answer, "How much are you willing to surrender to God?" One more question, "Do you really have faith that God can do all you ask?" The answer, "Are you willing to fast and ask God to give you mountain-moving faith?" (Mark 11:22-24).

Lord, forgive my doubts about Your ability to answer my prayers. Forgive my lack of bold-
ness in prayer. I pray with the disciples, "Increase my faith" (Luke 17:5). Amen.

Fasting is a spiritual discipline that gets you ready to meet God. Do you want the Holy Spirit to be poured on you? Fasting only gives you access to God; it is there you ask for the Holy Spirit. If you really want the Holy Spirit...fast...then go stand under the spout. That is where God pours out the Holy Spirit into your life. If you stand at the right spot, you will be poured on. If you open up a wide space in your heart, you will get a lot of Him. If you will start fasting right now, you will get Him sooner. Okay. Start fasting, then go stand under the spout.

Lord, I am not full...I am only partially filled. I will fast and pray and stand under the spout. I will do my part because I want the Holy Spirit poured on me. Amen.

READING:

Joel 2:12-32;

Acts 2:1-12

Key Thought: The Lord promises that when His people are spiritually ready and fast properly, He will pour the Holy Spirit on them.

REFLECTION

Day 20

GETTING READY

*"Moses proceeded to do everything just as the Lord had commanded him. …Then
the cloud covered the tabernacle, and the glory of the Lord filled the tabernacle."*

Exodus 40:16, 34, NLT

FASTING is an action to get you ready for a visit from God. In the 1988 movie *Field of Dreams*, a man kept hearing a voice, "If you build it, they will come." He built an amazing baseball field on his farm in the middle of Iowa, USA. Then many great Hall of Fame players of the past came to play baseball on the newly built field. In a parallel truth, if you prepare properly to worship the Lord, He will come to receive worship. In the Scripture reading for today, Moses built the tabernacle, "Just as the Lord had commanded him" (Ex. 40:16, NLT). He put everything in place where God instructed. The curtains were hung, the door was put in place, and then each piece of furniture in the tabernacle was placed in its location. When Moses obeyed and the tabernacle was built, God came. What do you have to do to get God to come to your life?

> *Lord, I have received Christ as my Savior, my sins are forgiven, and Christ lives in me. I am learning Your Word and trying to be a good testimony to family and friends, and I attend church, tithe, and try to serve You. Come.... Amen.*

Your fasting by itself is not enough. You must get things right with Jesus. Fasting is not to pleasure yourself. When you fast and get everything ready for the Lord, Jesus will come. When Moses put everything in place...the Glory Cloud came. When you put everything in place...God's presence will come. Repent from your private sins, immerse yourself in Scripture, pray for your family, friends and loved ones...serve God...tithe...then fast. When you put everything in place, God's presence will come.

Lord, I don't need more Bible knowledge...I need Your presence. I don't need to do more ministry, and I don't need to fast, and I don't need anything else. I need Your presence. I am getting my tabernacle ready...come...fill. Amen.

READING:

Exodus 40:1-38

Key Thought: The key to answered prayer is not fasting by itself. When you prepare your life as a tabernacle for God's presence, He will come to fill it.

REFLECTION

Day 21

WHEN FASTING IS GOOD

*"Esther sent this reply to Mordecai: 'Go and gather together all the
Jews of Susa and fast for me. Do not eat or drink for three days, night or
day. My maids and I will do the same. And then, though it is against
the law, I will go in to see the king. If I must die, I must die.'"*

Esther 4:15-16, NLT

A holocaust to kill every Jew in Persia was planned when Esther was queen. How did she face this emergency? She asked every Jew to fast with her. There were other occasions in Old Testament history when Israel fasted for emergencies, when a king asked everyone in the nation to fast to God for deliverance. Your answer to an emergency is not about what food you give up, and it's not about what you pray or how long you pray. The answer is about God. You get His attention when you give up necessary food to seek His presence. Added to that, you give up food that is delightful to find satisfaction in Him. Then fasting gets answers.

Jesus, You gave up everything for me. You left heaven and lived among humans and died for our sins. I will give my whole life for You. I will fast, pray, and put You first in everything. Amen.

Because Esther and the Jews fasted, the entire Jewish population was saved. Haman the evil prime minster who had plotted to eliminate all Jews was hanged on a gallows planned for Esther's uncle. God's justice was quick and surprising. Esther's uncle, Mordecai, was hated by Hamon, was made prime minister in Hamon's place.

Lord, remind me to fast when I face dangers. The answer is in You, not in the foods I give up or the length of my fast. The greater the danger, the longer I will fast. I will demonstrate my faith by my fast. Amen.

READING:

Esther 4:1-17

Key Thought: When Queen Esther faced a threat against her life and all the other Jews in Persia, she called on all of Israel to fast for deliverance and God answered.

REFLECTION

Appendix

QUESTIONS AND ANSWERS ABOUT FASTING *

1. WHY SHOULD I ENTER A FAST?

YOU don't begin fasting for the sake of fasting, you fast for a deeper purpose. Usually, a person will fast for a prayer request that is extremely urgent or a prayer request too difficult to get an answer by prayer alone. God has given to us the avenue of praying daily to Him. He has invited us, "Ask, and it shall be given you; seek, and ye shall find; knock, and it shall be opened unto you" (Matthew 7:7, KJV). The word for *asking* in the original language is in the continuous tense; it means keep on asking. But sometimes you pray constantly, and the answer does not come. That is the time to fast.

2. MUST I ALWAYS NEED A REASON TO FAST?

No, some Christians have made it a habit in their Christian discipline to fast one or more days a week. An evangelist fasted every Friday. Many people didn't understand why he was so effective in winning people to Christ. He got results that others couldn't get. He could turn almost any conversation into a soul-winning event. The evangelist never told what he did to get results, but he fasted every Friday for souls.

On some Fridays he fasted for certain individuals, calling them by name before the heavenly Father. Also he fasted on Fridays for certain situations where he would speak or hold evangelistic meetings. He prayed,

---

*Material in this chapter taken from *Fasting Can Change Your Life*, by Jerry Falwell and Elmer L. Towns, Regal Books, Ventura, CA, 1998, 252-273.

fasted, and asked God to use those meetings that the lost might get saved.

But there may be other occasions when you fast without a purpose. Many believers have fasted just to worship God. They do not have a crucial need, nor do they have a crisis in their life. They have learned that God makes Himself more real to them when they fast.

First, you will discipline yourself to fast once a week to worship God. There was an individual who set aside most Mondays to fast as worship to God. He began at sundown on Sunday, eating before he went to evening church on the Lord's Day. During the church service he began his fast, and after church service, if he ever went out for fellowship with individuals, all he took was a liquid to drink. This individual fasted most Mondays as an act of worship to God. It so happened that he was off work on Mondays and could devote longer times for worshipping, longer times to reading Scriptures, and longer times to meditating on the Lord.

Second, others will set aside a certain day to fast and meditate on God. A minister traveled far from home for several meetings. He finished a speaking engagement on Wednesday night and then did not have another meeting until Friday; so he set aside Thursday to fast and fellowship with God. This fasting day was not for specific prayer requests but just to fellowship with God, to worship God, and to enjoy God.

3. WHAT IS A SUGGESTED SEQUENCE FOR PRAYER AND WORSHIP DURING A DAY OF FASTING?

First, spend time reading several psalms, specifically looking for those psalms that are prayers to God.

Next, pray these psalms to God either in worship, thanksgiving, or adoration.

Then read several epistles. Do this with pen in hand, underlining the names of Christ, the key words of the book or some other item. Usually, Paul's letters have prayers, so pray these prayers. Also, when fasting, try to read a large portion of the Bible about the life of Christ. Since Christ is our example, your desire is to be like Christ.

Next, pray the Lord's Prayer several times. It is recommended that everyone pray daily the Lord's Prayer.

Then go back through your last three or four months of prayer requests, asking God to answer those requests that have not been answered. Finally, survey the list of answered prayers in the last four months. Record those under the praise section. Use these answers as a catalyst to worship God, thank God, and adore Him for what He has done.

4. HOW LONG SHOULD I FAST THE FIRST TIME?

Begin with the normal fast, i.e., going without solid food for one day. Don't start off with a 3-day fast, a 7-day fast, and surely not a 40-day fast. If you start off with a longer fast and something happens that you don't complete it, you'll get discouraged and lose trust in your abilities. Then you've accomplished the opposite for which you fast. You've weakened your discipline rather than strengthening it. Start with what you can do, a one-day normal fast.

5. WHAT KIND OF FAST IS BEST FOR THE FIRST TIME?

Begin with a Yom Kippur fast, which is a 24-hour fast recognizing the way God puts limits on days. The Yom Kippur fast begins at sundown the first day, and extends to sundown the following day, i.e. twenty-four hours. Remember in the Creation how God divided the days, "the evening and the morning were the second day" (Genesis 1:8, NKJV). So, eat a small item before sundown and fast the evening meal. The next day fast breakfast and lunch. Then after the sun goes down, eat dinner.

6. WHAT SHOULD I WITHHOLD DURING MY FIRST FAST?

There are several different ways to fast. First is the absolute fast where you withhold solid food and water. Do not start with an absolute fast. The absolute fast is seldom mentioned in the Bible, and it is usually identified with supernatural help from God, i.e. a miracle. It is impossible for the human body to normally function over a period of time without water. The body dehydrates, and it loses brain cells. To go without water is dangerous. I have known people who have gone three days without water, but it is not recommended. People who have gone seven days without water probably have some physical damage done to them.

Begin with a normal fast, withholding solid food but drinking liquids. If after several normal fasts God leads you to a one-day absolute fast or even a 3-day, make sure it is the leadership of God. Make sure that you are not doing it out of guilt, pride to make a statement, or any other reason of the flesh. Make sure it is the Spirit of God that is leading you in this undertaking.

7. IS IT A FAST IF I DON'T COMPLETELY ABSTAIN FROM FOOD?

Some non-Christians have different combinations of fasts. One religion (not Christianity) will have a 40-day fast in which they will not eat during the day; they eat only eat after sundown and before sunup.

Some Christians have been led to abstain from one meal a day, using that time to pray and worship God. They eat the other two meals a day. This could be a valid fast.

A lady didn't eat breakfast and lunch because she was fasting for her unsaved family. Her unsaved family had told they didn't want her doing "religious things" like fasting to try to convert them. She did not tell them she was fasting for them during breakfast and lunch. She prepared the evening meal and ate it with them, with the intent of not offending, but lovingly attempting to win them to Christ.

8. IS IT A FAST IF I MODIFY MY DIET TO ABSTAIN FROM SOME FOOD, WHILE EATING OTHER FOOD?

John Wesley practiced what we call the "Wesley Fast." John Wesley fasted ten days, eating only whole grain bread and water. Wesley fasting primarily for his ministerial students. It was during this time he was preparing sermons to preach to the lay ministers who were in charge of early Methodist parishes. Many of these men did not have education and John Wesley, George Whitfield, Charles Wesley, and others preached one sermon after another to them. Then these lay pastors went out and preached those same sermons to their churches. As Wesley spent his time praying and fasting, God reached England through these ministers. It was the beginning of the First Great Awakening that spread around the world.

The next partial fast is called the Daniel Fast where he demonstrated that he could be healthier than others by only eating vegetables. Apparently, Daniel didn't eat any meat or other items from the king's tables (this might have involved alcoholic beverages, or even food that had been offered to demonic idols). But in any case, Daniel entered into a partial fast eating only vegetables. On another occasion Daniel said, "I ate no pleasant bread, neither came flesh nor wine in my mouth, neither did I anoint myself at all, till three whole weeks were fulfilled" (Daniel 10:3, NKJV). This apparently was a partial fast of enjoyable food, such as desserts.

9. SHOULD I FAST IF I HAVE MEDICAL PROBLEMS?

There are many medical problems that would disqualify a person from fasting, such as a person with diabetes, a pregnant woman, a nursing woman, etc. One medical doctor indicated there are about 30 pathologies that should disqualify a person from fasting.

God would not ask persons to do something (fast) that would physically harm themselves. God never asks us to mutilate the body, mark the body, harm the body, or in any type of aestheticism, damage the body.

First, people with a medical problem should treat food as a prescription or medicine. They can eat during mealtimes, but commit themselves to prayer and join "in spirit" with others in the fast. When persons with medical problems eat, obviously they would stay away from delightful food, enjoyable food, and only eat that which is basic and necessary for their health.

Second, people with medical problems make a vow to pray when they can't make a vow to abstain from food. God knows they physically can't fast, but if those persons pray as diligently as those fasting, God will join their faith to the others for an answer. Through the years God used a number of diabetics with the right attitude, who felt their prayers were just effective because of the spirit of their fast, even though they ate enough to "accommodate" their medical problem.

Some diabetics have believed they must "trust God," stop eating as an act of faith, and fast to God. While they sincerely hold this view, they don't realize what harm they do to their bodies. It is questionable if a diabetic person should leave food that is necessary for good health. They must be absolutely sure their step of faith is prescribed by God. Many have taken that step of faith presumptuously or they were self-deceived.

Because it is so easy to be self-deceived, you should err on the side of safety. Eat a little to keep your physical health. Remember the "law of silence," i.e., when God has not spoken, don't make rules for yourself or others. Since God is silent in the area of the sick person fasting, let us not make a rule to eat or not to eat. Rather, recognize the physical mandate of the body; let us eat and pray.

10. IS IT POSSIBLE TO BE NEUROTIC AND FAST?

Some people have a wrong attitude toward food. They feel that anything that is enjoyable is sin, so anything they like to do must be wrong. They feel since food is necessary and enjoyable, they are giving in to sin when they eat. Therefore, such a person may think that fasting is spiritual, and just refraining from food itself will make them godlier. This attitude is wrong, it is not refraining from food that makes us spiritual. Fasting gives us time for the heart to respond to God; that makes us spiritual.

For the person who is neurotic about food, remember the great feasts in the Old Testament. God's people were commanded to come to Jerusalem and celebrate the Feast of Passover, the Feast of Weeks, and the other great feasts during the Jewish calendar year. When a Jewish believer brought his peace offering to God, the animal was roasted on the brazen altar and the Levite (priest) and the worshiper together sat down to eat an old-fashioned "Georgia" Bar-B-Que. They ate the food together in enjoyment and worship to God. (The sin and trespass offerings were burnt completely because of a person's sin, but the peace offering was a time of fellowship). As a general rule, God made more provisions for feasts than for fasting.

As you come into the New Testament you see Jesus coming to a marriage feast. It doesn't say He ate, but He probably did. He ate at the home of Matthew, and Zacchaeus, and He ate the Feast of Passover with His disciples the night before He died. There are occasions of Paul having a fellowship meal with the Christians, and in the early church they enjoyed a love feast before they served the elements at the Lord's Table. No, it is not wrong to eat. This is a gift that God has given to us and those who say we should not eat, misinterpret scripture. Remember Paul said, "Let no man therefore judge you in meat, nor in drink, or in respect of a holy day . . ." (Colossians 2:16, KJV).

11. CAN I FAST AND STILL GO TO WORK?

Yes, it is possible to fast and still work an eight hour day. Because, most people work around unsaved people, perhaps it is not best to announce to your fellow workers that you are fasting that day. Remember the words of Jesus who said, "When ye fast, be not as the hypocrites, of a sad countenance: for they disfigure their faces that they may appear unto men to fast. Verily I say unto you, they have their reward. But thou, when thou fastest, anoint thine head and wash thy face; that thou not appear unto men to fast, but to thy Father which is in secret: and the Father which is in secret shall reward thee openly" (Matthew 6:16-18, KJV).

This verse tells you a couple of things. Don't needlessly tell people you are fasting. Especially when you are fasting for a private matter. But rather, you should appear as you do any other day. Therefore, when you are fasting at work, ladies should make sure to put on makeup as other days. Men should make sure they are shaven, and their hair is combed so people do not know what they are doing. Why? Because you are fasting to the Father in heaven. He will see and answer.

12. CAN I FAST IF I HAVE BUSINESS OR PERSONAL RESPONSIBILITIES?

Yes, many have fasted and attended lunch meetings and/or other occasions where there was eating. They did not feel any obligation to eat a meal, just because they went to a business meeting in a restaurant where food is served. There have been other occasions where some have eaten before arriving at a business meeting or have had an upset stomach and didn't feel like eating; therefore, do not be intimated when you are fasting and called to such a meeting. When the server comes to you simply say, "I'll just take coffee."

I do not make a big deal of it. I do not explain to anyone what I am doing. I just take coffee. If someone asks why I am not eating, I say simply, "I just want coffee."

You should fast in secret when you have a private request or for private worship. It is a time when you do not advertise your fast. Remember what Jesus said, "That thou appear not unto men to fast, but unto thy Father which is in secret, and thy Father which seeth in secret, shall reward thee openly" (Matthew 6:18, KJV).

14. WHAT CAN I DRINK DURING A FAST?

The question of drinking is debatable. In Korea, an American Christian mentioned he drank coffee during fasting. Many of the Koreans were upset at his suggestion; they felt that one should only drink water. On another occasion he was speaking to a Southern Baptist associational meeting in a large southern city. He mentioned that he would drink coffee during his fasts and one of the delegates was upset. From the floor he yelled an objection,

"Coffee is a stimulant and you shouldn't drink it during a fast."

His answer was very simple when he said that coffee is a stimulant and can make you hungry, but he drank it anyway.

"But...," the objector continued, "coffee has caffeine that will stimulate you physically." He went on to say you shouldn't do anything to stimulate the physical body but rather afflict yourself and feel weakness that comes by fasting.

Some people drink only fruit or vegetable juices when fasting. Some say fresh fruits or vegetables are best because they do not have salt or seasonings that are found in canned juice or in a commercial product like V-8. A leading advocate of fasting indicates that once a day he gets a blender and blends vegetables into juice, then drinks that for sustenance. Drinking fruit or vegetable juice is not the same as eating and enjoying the chewing and munching factor. Some drink V-8 juice on long fasts. Again, the law of silence applies here. *Where God has not spoken, don't make rules.*

An elderly man drank a small can of Ensure, which is a balanced protein supplement drink. This elderly man did not eat normal meals, did not drink enjoyable liquids, but took one can of Ensure each day. Again, the law of silence applies here. *When God has not spoken, don't make rules.*

Many people who have fasted for 40 days have been asked what they drink. They say they drink Diet Pepsi, Slim Fast, grape juice, and a number of other products. At one seminar, someone complained the Slim Fast didn't constitute a biblical 40-day fast. They replied, "Until you go without food for 40 days and drink only one Slim Fast a day, don't complain."

15. IS THE 40-DAY FAST POSSIBLE TODAY?

Many thought a 40-day fast was not possible. They might say a 40-day fast was taught in the Bible, but probably not for today.

Yes, a 40-day fast is possible today. Many have fasted for 40 days. There have been thousands of people who have joined Bill Bright in fasting 40 days for national revival and a national return to the Judeo-Christian ethic.

16. CAN FASTING BE LEGALISM?

Anything in the Christian life can be done legalistically. Legalism is attempting to keep a rule for spiritual results. Therefore you can repeat the Lord's Prayer legalistically, thinking that by the mere repetition of words you will become godlier. Or, you can give money to God legalistically. Legalism involves the outer obedience without the inner response of the heart. A person can legalistically stay sexually pure yet in his heart by lustful and tempted to fornication.

Therefore, fasting can be legalistic. There have been people who have used fasting to make a bargain with God. "If I don't eat food, will you save my husband?" This is only one example. People have asked for healing, money, deliverance, and all other types of answers, simply because they fasted.

You can legalistically be baptized, attend church, tithe, and do all of the other things a Christian is supposed to do. However, just because you think your attitude is wrong that does not give you the freedom to refuse baptism or to refuse going to church. Rather, you must get your inward heart right with God then obey outwardly; that is God's requirement.

Because fasting can be legalistic, it doesn't mean you should never fast because of your fear of legalism. Rather get right with God, approach fasting with the right heart attitude, and withhold food for the right purpose.

17. CAN YOU FAST FOR MORE THAN ONE PRAYER REQUEST AT A TIME?

Some think it is not a true fast if you are fasting for all the things on your prayer request list. They think it is not fasting if you have several prayer requests. In one sense, you usually fast for one compelling thing but still pray for the other items on your prayer list. A study of the original meaning of the word fast will give some insight. The word *fast* comes from the verb *tsome,* i.e. a word associated with emergency or

distress. When a soldier is in the middle of a battle fighting for his life, he doesn't stop to have tea or breakfast. In his struggle he doesn't even think about food. In the same way, when you are struggling for spiritual survival, you don't think about food, you just want to pray and not even take time to eat a meal. That is the true nature of fasting.

Think of a man lost in a snowstorm, a family trapped in their van in a flood, or the time you heard someone you loved had died. In the middle of the emergency you don't think of visiting the hamburger stand to get something to eat. You surely don't want French fries or a milkshake. You want deliverance and you are yelling in your heart,

"Help!!!."

Therefore, the person who is fasting and praying, does not usually attach all his prayer requests to the fast. In the true sense of fasting, we pray for one deep burden.

Some people do without food, putting themselves back into the mental state of an emergency. This is why the Bible associates, "afflicting one's soul and body" (2 Samuel 3:25, ELT) with fasting.

18. WHAT HAPPENS IF YOU VIOLATE YOUR FAST?

There is a difference between breaking your fast and violating your fast. You break your fast when you reach the time "vow" of your fasting. When you come to a natural conclusion, you stop. Many people fast for one day and do not eat until the sun comes up the following day. Therefore they break their fast with a meal called "breakfast."

To violate one's fast is to eat during the time when you have made a vow to God not to eat. This can happen voluntarily or involuntarily.

A man walked to his office manager's desk during the Halloween season. There was candy corn in a dish on her desk. He was fasting for a lengthy fast and never even realized what he was doing. He reached into her candy dish, picked up two or three candy corns, and popped them into his mouth. After about the third candy corn, it dawned on him he was fasting and that he had just violated his fast.

He confessed to the secretary what he had just done. He went back to his office and confessed to God that he had not kept his vow to Him. While not intentional, he had broken the spirit of his fast and was not willing to continue his fast. That evening he took a meal and continued eating for the next two or three days. Then, he entered into the fast that he had originally begun before violating it. The second time he carried the fast through to conclusion.

Others have intentionally violated their fast. They just couldn't hold out; they needed a hamburger or they wanted to eat a meal with the family. Like all other vows that are made, the fast is a vow. Therefore, God gives a pattern how to treat vows that are not kept.

First, recognize it as a violation.

Second, ask God's forgiveness.

Third, recognize that you have hurt your self-esteem because you did not keep a promise you made to yourself and to God.

Fourth, purpose to enter into another fast at another time so you can do what you have committed yourself to originally do.

People who have violated their fast should not to make a big deal out of it. Confess it, and put it behind you. Learn a lesson from it, and go on to the next event in your life.

19. WHAT IS GLUTTONY?

The dictionary definition of *gluttony* is "one given habitually to greedy and voracious drinking and eating, a great capacity for accepting or enduring punishment."

Gluttony is more than the volume of food or repetition with which we eat food. Gluttony can express itself in a "slavish" interest in the entire experience of food, smelling, tasting, eating, enjoying, etc. The gluttonous person is one who lives on the level of his appetite and driven by his physical appetite.

While fasting focus your mind on the good things that God has given us, God has also given us food for health, strength and the enjoyable experiences of life. Those who don't eat properly, get the opposite, which is illness, nausea and even mental problems.

When you fast, focus your mind on the good things God has given to you. Remember, "do not work for food that spoils," said Jesus, "but for food that endures to eternal life, which the Son of Man will give you" (John 6:27, NIV). While you are fasting, perhaps the Daniel Fast will lead you to understand how enjoyable a simple vegetable can be.

Fasting is not about withholding food but about seeking God and His will, because the true meaning of spiritual hunger drives us to know God. Your hunger should point you to God, who satisfies.

20. WHAT ABOUT SECOND-GUESSING YOURSELF ONCE YOU BEGIN A FAST?

On several occasions when people "re-think" their terms of their fast vows after they begin, the most common problem are those who have added additional "vows" after they have begun their fast. As an illustration, some who have begun fasting then have added an additional abstention, such as fasting from golf, fasting from television, fasting from sex with their marriage partner, fasting from attending sporting events, fasting from reading newspapers, etc.

Why have some people added extra vows to their fast?

First, they sometimes hear about how others have fasted from some additional items they didn't include.

Second, some feel guilty enjoying themselves while fasting.

Third, some didn't realize what they were getting into when they began fasting. When they got into spiritual warfare, they got scared, then upped the ante, adding a lot more items of sacrifice to their fast.

Fourth, some were not clear or concise when they began to fast. Then as they took the fasting journey, some began eating things that made them guilty, i.e., cream soups or mashed fruits, instead of fruit juice, etc. Others who didn't have clear fasting objectives and clear fasting vows, began adding other requirements, such as one who said he stopped drinking fruit juice because it was too enjoyable.

A fifth was a person who began fasting for a request, but when there was no movement toward an answer, this person decided he was not doing enough, so he quit watching TV, listening to the radio or CD music, and taking enjoyable walks in the woods.

As you look at the above who have "re-thought" their fast, it seems some of their motivations have been "works," i.e., doing something or doing more to please God. Fasting should be motivated by grace; you can never offer God any bargaining chip to get Him to answer a prayer. God answers when you hunger and thirst after Him, more than hungering after things in this world.

But others have "re-thought" their vow, perhaps because of a psychological weakness. It could be a weak ego, a negative self-perception, or even some emotional problems. When some don't have the emotional strength to make a decision/vow and then stick to that decision, they could very well change their minds about what they have yielded to God.

Finally, others have changed their minds about fasting because they didn't understand the nature of fasting when they began or they weren't clear in their commitment when they began.

NOTES

PART FIVE

21 DAYS OF
PRAYER AND FASTING

ADDITIONAL RESOURCES

POWERPOINT SLIDES:

To purchase and download the Powerpoint Slides go to
https://www.norimediagroup.com/pages/elmer-towns

VIDEO:

To purchase available video by Dr Towns go to
https://www.norimediagroup.com/pages/elmer-towns

ADD-ON CONTENT

To purchase additional products in this series go to
https://www.norimediagroup.com/pages/elmer-towns

RELATED BOOKS

Available at https://www.norimediagroup.com/pages/elmer-towns

www.ingramcontent.com/pod-product-compliance
Lightning Source LLC
Chambersburg PA
CBHW060118120726
48003CB00009B/2692